The 5 Minute

PRAYER
PLAN

Print ISBN 978-1-68322-462-4

Published by Barbour Books, an imprint of Barbour Publishing, Inc., 1810 Barbour Drive, Uhrichsville, Ohio 44683, www.barbourbooks.com

Our mission is to inspire the world with the life-changing message of the Bible.

Printed in the United States of America.

The 5 Minute

PRAYER PLAN

A Guide to More Focused Prayer

Shanna D. Gregor

BARBOUR BOOKS
An Imprint of Barbour Publishing, Inc.

INTRODUCTION

Prayer is meant to be a dynamic exchange between the majestic Creator and His creation. No doubt you've experienced those moments of divine connection at different seasons in your life, and yet you still at times fall into a repetitious routine where you just want your time in prayer to be more but aren't sure how to get there.

This practical and inspirational book will open up new ways into prayer with more than ninety "5-minute" plans for your daily quiet time. You'll explore prayer plans focused on various aspects of life, such as health, finances, forgiveness, grace, witnessing to others, worry, thankfulness, protection, work, relationships, church, government, and the future. A handy subject index in the back of the book will help you find these topics quickly.

Each entry includes:

- Minute 1: a scripture to meditate on
- Minutes 2-3: specific prayer points and questions to consider as you enter a time of prayer
- Minutes 4-5: a jump-starter prayer to springboard you into a time of conversation with God

The prayers in this book have been written with you in mind, each word penned in prayer, asking the Lord to give insight into the needs of those who will pick up this book and begin a new or renewed journey with Him. Deep, heartfelt prayer happens in those quiet moments when you stand transparently before the One with arms wide open to embrace you in unconditional love.

BUILDING THROUGH PRAYER

,,,

*But you, dear friends, must build up your lives ever more
strongly upon the foundation of our holy faith, learning to pray
in the power and strength of the Holy Spirit. Stay always within
the boundaries where God's love can reach and bless you.
Wait patiently for the eternal life that our Lord Jesus Christ
in his mercy is going to give you. Try to help those who argue
against you. Be merciful to those who doubt. Save some by
snatching them as from the very flames of hell itself. And as
for others, help them to find the Lord by being kind to them,
but be careful that you yourselves aren't pulled along
into their sins. Hate every trace of their sin
while being merciful to them as sinners.*

Jude 20–23 TLB

,,,

- Jude encourages you to fight for your faith. How do you contend for your faith each day?
- Have you ever been exposed to false doctrine?
- When faced with counterfeits, how do you recognize the truth?
- Your reputation is important to your faith. How do you protect your reputation?
- Do others see you as a witness of Christ?
- How do you point others to Christ through your own story?
- When have you failed to point others to Christ? How can you recover from that?
- How do you wait patiently for the eternal life you've been promised?

Heavenly Father, today I build myself upon my most holy faith, praying in the Spirit as You speak to my heart and help me to believe and receive those things that You've prepared for me. Help me to recognize Your truth and turn away from the enemy's attempts to deceive me. Give me a spirit of discernment. Give me wisdom, understanding, and love as I live each day in a way that points others to You. Give me words to say in every situation so that I may live a life that is a witness to others of Your goodness and love. Thank You for Your power and strength to embrace those things that grow my faith. Let others see You in me today.

FAITH FOR THE FAMILY

,,

When the jailer, shaken out of sleep, saw the prison doors open, he drew his sword and was about to kill himself, thinking that the prisoners had escaped. But Paul shouted, saying, "Do not hurt yourself, we are all here!" Then the jailer called for torches and rushed in, and trembling with fear he fell down before Paul and Silas, and after he brought them out [of the inner prison], he said, "Sirs, what must I do to be saved?" And they answered, "Believe in the Lord Jesus [as your personal Savior and entrust yourself to Him] and you will be saved, you and your household [if they also believe]." And they spoke the word of the Lord [concerning eternal salvation through faith in Christ] to him and to all who were in his house.

ACTS 16:27-32 AMP

,,

- What does family mean to you?
- When the jailer in today's scripture asked to be saved, Paul and Silas extended the invitation to his household. What influence do you have in your relationships?
- Have you found it difficult to share Christ with your family members? Even some of Jesus' own family didn't believe.
- What struggles have you had with your family and those you love?
- How has your family influenced you in your faith?
- What are your hopes and dreams for those you love?

Lord, family is important to me, and I know it is important to You. Sometimes past pain or family history tries to drive a wedge between those relationships. Give me wisdom to know how to navigate the difficult ones. Thank You for the relationships You've placed in my life. Show me the purpose of each relationship. Help me to hear the words of wisdom from those You speak through. Give me wisdom for others as we walk out this life together. Help me to respond to them as You would. Give me an overwhelming love for others and a desire for them to know You intimately.

BLESSED TO GIVE

••

Blessed is the man who walks not in the counsel of the ungodly, nor stands in the path of sinners, nor sits in the seat of the scornful; but his delight is in the law of the LORD, and in His law he meditates day and night. He shall be like a tree planted by the rivers of water, that brings forth its fruit in its season, whose leaf also shall not wither; and whatever he does shall prosper. . . . "You shall surely give to him, and your heart should not be grieved when you give to him, because for this thing the LORD your God will bless you in all your works and in all to which you put your hand."

PSALM 1:1–3; DEUTERONOMY 15:10 NKJV

••

- Do you consider yourself to be a generous person?
- Do you think blessing means to walk free and clear of difficulty or failure? Why or why not?
- Has difficulty brought blessing into your life? How?
- Have you experienced increase because of the favor of God on your life?
- In what ways has He increased you—financially or otherwise?
- What are your dreams for your financial future?
- As God blesses you financially, what plans do you have for that increase?
- Often the thought of blessing immediately goes to finances, but in what other ways has your relationship with God allowed you to bless others?

*Lord, I am blessed because I have a
relationship with You. You bless me because
You love me. I am Your child. Your favor
goes before me, and I receive Your promise
that everything I put my hand to is blessed
because of my relationship with You. As I
honor You with my life, with my decisions, and
with my increase, please show me how to be
generous and hold those blessings loosely.
Give me wisdom in how to invest the things
You entrust me with both in this world and
in Your kingdom. I have the mind of Christ
in all things. I think His thoughts and
respond to His direction in all I do.*

WAITING—STANDING FIRM IN THE IN-BETWEEN TIMES

◦◦

*I will stand at my guard post. I will station myself on the wall.
I will watch to see what he will say to me and what answer I
will get to my complaint. Then the LORD answered me,
"Write the vision. Make it clear on tablets so that anyone
can read it quickly. The vision will still happen at the appointed
time. It hurries toward its goal. It won't be a lie. If it's delayed,
wait for it. It will certainly happen. It won't be late. Look at
the proud person. He is not right in himself. But the righteous
person will live because of his faithfulness."*

HABAKKUK 2:1–4 GW

◦◦

- Has God asked you to do something, but it's not yet time to move forward?
- Do you find it difficult to wait? Why?
- What answers are you waiting on?
- It can be challenging when you know God wants you to do something but you're waiting for the next step. How do you trust God during the in-between time?
- Spending time in God's Word can help keep discouragement and doubt at bay while waiting. What scriptures encourage you to wait?
- What "if onlys" is the enemy challenging you with?
- What promises has God given you to stand in faith against those "if onlys"?
- What things in your past are holding you back or causing you to doubt God's faithfulness?
- What thoughts do you need to change in order to let go of those thoughts and trust Him?

Heavenly Father, I believe I have heard from You and accept what You have prepared for me. I hate to wait, but I know Your timing is best. Today I choose to wait with patience. Please help me when I become discouraged and doubt Your promises. Forgive me when I become uncertain and feel like maybe I didn't hear from You. Give me strength to stand strong and believe the new things You are doing in my life. Right now I don't see it, but I hold on and believe, because when I trust You, the rewards are great. Wash away the past that sometimes haunts me. I consciously choose to throw away those "if onlys" and take Your hand. Guide me safely through this in-between season of my life as I study Your Word and believe Your truth!

IN THE FACE OF ADVERSITY

*I waited and waited and waited for GOD. At last he looked;
finally he listened. He lifted me out of the ditch, pulled me
from deep mud. He stood me up on a solid rock to make sure
I wouldn't slip. He taught me how to sing the latest God-song,
a praise-song to our God. More and more people are seeing
this: they enter the mystery, abandoning themselves to GOD.
Blessed are you who give yourselves over to GOD,
turn your backs on the world's "sure thing,"
ignore what the world worships.*

PSALM 40:1–4 MSG

- When you feel lost and alone, do your thoughts turn
  to God?
- What brings you comfort and confirms that God knows your
  pain?
- How do you know God has heard your heart cry, even when
  you don't feel like He has?
- What thought do you battle while trying to stay focused on
  what God has promised?
- When you feel like God doesn't hear you or that He's not
  listening to you, what settles your heart?
- What part does praise play in your rescue from the prison of
  adversity?
- When have you faced adversity and God rescued you?
- What things have you endured that looked impossible, and
  yet God turned them to your good?

You are the God of my salvation. You always and continually deliver me from the hand of my enemy. When I am weak, You are my strength. When I sit in silence, feeling alone, deep in my heart I know I am not alone. You are with me. You have a purpose for all of this, and I choose to wait for Your plan to be revealed. I can't see it now, but I know You will use this situation for my good. I will stand firm in faith. I remember the times You've saved me. I remind my soul how You always and forever bring me into a place of favor and blessing. I will not waver. I will wait for You to lift me up from this situation and place me firmly in a spacious place. I trust You, Lord. I praise You even when I don't feel like it. I will rise, eventually, above all of this by Your holy hand.

WHEN YOUR HEART HURTS

My tears have been my food day and night, while people say to me all day long, "Where is your God?"... Why, my soul, are you downcast? Why so disturbed within me? Put your hope in God, for I will yet praise him, my Savior and my God. My soul is downcast within me; therefore I will remember you from the land of the Jordan, the heights of Hermon—from Mount Mizar.

PSALM 42:3, 5-6 NIV

- How do you respond when those heavy hurts and disappointments in life confront you?
- If you wear your emotions on your sleeve, does that impact those you love in a positive or negative way?
- When those negative thoughts seem to outweigh the positive ones, do you turn to others for help? Do you look to God?
- Do you have someone you can talk to? Perhaps a spiritual leader or faithful friend?
- When was the last time you poured out your heart to God? Did you express what you felt honestly to Him?
- What questions do you still want to ask God?
- What actions can you take that you know help lift the heaviness?
- How has God been faithful in the past? And how do those experiences help you now?
- What things can you do to encourage yourself in the Lord?
- What scriptures can you think of that will help you take your mind off present situations and offer you hope?

Lord, my heart is hurting. I can't help but feel discouraged and disappointed. You know all that has happened and how much I've endured. I don't know how much more I can take. I need Your help. Thank You that I don't have to navigate this journey by myself. Remind me of the great things You have done in my life. Bring those amazing moments to my remembrance. More times than I can count, I know You have saved me. You comforted me and granted me peace. You said in this world we would have trouble. I know You will not allow more than I can bear, but it's hard. Give me peace and strength to stand firm. Help me to believe You are at work in this situation. I know that no matter how bad it looks right now, You can turn the situation around. I receive hope as I take a deep breath and refocus on You.

CONFIDENCE IN GOD'S PROTECTION

,,

Give us help against the enemy, for the help of man is worthless
(ineffectual, without purpose). Through God we will have victory,
for He will trample down our enemies. . . . Hear my cry, O God;
listen to my prayer. From the end of the earth I call to You, when
my heart is overwhelmed and weak; lead me to the rock that is
higher than I [a rock that is too high to reach without Your help].
For You have been a shelter and a refuge for me, a strong
tower against the enemy. Let me dwell in Your tent forever;
let me take refuge in the shelter of Your wings. Selah.

PSALM 60:11–12; 61:1–4 AMP

,,

- Like the psalmist, do you have feelings of fear about those who want to hurt you?
- How can you turn your adverse surroundings into encouraging reminders of God's faithful existence in your life?
- Do you spend a lot of time worrying about what might happen?
- How can you better manage stresses you're experiencing by first praising God?
- What internal, emotional hurts do you fear? How are you guarding your heart?
- Are there areas of your heart you've kept for yourself that perhaps need to be given to God for safekeeping?
- When you've called to God in the past, has He answered?
- How many different situations can you recall in the next few minutes where God spared you from an accident, kept you from a dangerous situation, or saved you from a disastrous outcome?
- Can you build your confidence in God's protection by reminding yourself of the many times He has responded to your cry for help?

*Heavenly Father, sometimes I am afraid.
We live in a messed-up world. Bad things
happen to those I consider good. It's difficult
for me to understand. I know that You hold my
life in Your hands. My time is not my own but
Yours, and yet I desire a long life filled with
Your goodness and love. Forgive me when
I've closed certain areas of my heart to You.
Today I choose to open them wide for You
to keep. When I call, You always answer.
When I feel I am fighting a battle alone,
give me assurance that You are with me.
Give me wisdom to be in the right place at
the right time. I will follow close to You.
Hide me from my enemies and
keep me in safety next to You.*

HEALING COUNSELOR

‖‖‖

*All praise to the God and Father of our Master, Jesus the
Messiah! Father of all mercy! God of all healing counsel!
He comes alongside us when we go through hard times,
and before you know it, he brings us alongside someone else
who is going through hard times so that we can be there for
that person just as God was there for us. We have plenty
of hard times that come from following the Messiah,
but no more so than the good times of his healing
comfort—we get a full measure of that, too.*

2 Corinthians 1:3–5 msg

‖‖‖

- No matter where you come from or who you are, life brings
  some sorrow. When have you felt great sorrow? Have you
  lost a loved one? Have you experienced loss of health,
  relationship, wealth, or job security? Have you experienced
  a difficult childhood, abandonment, disappointment, or
  broken dreams?
- Most likely those close to you were at a loss for words or
  said things they wish they could take back. What words
  have hurt your heart?
- When have you felt no one understood?
- One person does understand—Jesus. How do you think Jesus
  experienced great sorrow during His time on earth?
- Do you believe Jesus cares about what you're going
  through?
- Jesus is not intimidated by the hard questions your heart
  wants to ask during your pain. What questions do you want
  to ask Him?
- How are you listening for Jesus' reply?

Jesus, You know my sorrow, my grief, my pain. You know the words that have hurt my heart and the sense of loss I feel. No one truly understands my heart but You. I have a lot of questions I want to know the answers to, and perhaps those answers can only come from You. Lead me in the way I should go.

Show me the path that is right, because sometimes I am blinded by my grief. Give me strength to hear the truth in love. Help me to understand the hard things my heart needs to hear. Hold me tight as I let the tears fall. Wash away the brokenness. Thank You for Your counsel. Give me patience to hear all that You have to say. Touch my heart in the deep places where my emotions have been damaged and need healing that only You can bring. Help me to let go of the pain and say goodbye to all the hurts. Show me how to look at this experience through Your eyes. Pour out Your healing ointment and fill me with Your peace.

REVIVE US, O LORD

||||||||||||||||||||||||||||||||||||||||||||||||||||||||||||||||||||||||||||||

Return, we beseech You, O God of hosts; look down from heaven and see, and visit this vine and the vineyard which Your right hand has planted, and the branch that You made strong for Yourself. It is burned with fire, it is cut down; they perish at the rebuke of Your countenance. Let Your hand be upon the man of Your right hand, upon the son of man whom You made strong for Yourself. Then we will not turn back from You; revive us, and we will call upon Your name. Restore us, O LORD God of hosts; cause Your face to shine, and we shall be saved!

Psalm 80:14–19 NKJV

||||||||||||||||||||||||||||||||||||||||||||||||||||||||||||||||||||||||||||||

- What does revival mean to you?
- Revival begins when God's people recognize their need to be spiritually restored and revitalized. When did you realize you needed revitalization in your own personal walk with Jesus?
- Is your relationship with God everything you want it to be?
- What distractions cause your relationship with Him to grow cold?
- As God's child, the same Spirit that raised Christ from the dead lives in you. How do you stir up resurrection life in your heart?
- What God-given gifts do you recognize within your own heart? Are you actively in pursuit of Him so that those gifts can be used?
- What makes you hungry for more of God?
- What inspires you to share God's truths with others?
- How has God changed you?

God, Your hand is upon my life. I see You at work, and I know You have plans that I've not yet realized. I am grateful for Your love and Your mercy. I know there is so much more than I see that You have for me. I don't want to miss anything You have for me. I want to know You more. I want to go deeper in my relationship with You. Stir up Your life in me. Give me a desire for revitalization in my soul. Help me to recognize those distractions in life that keep me from reaching those goals You want me to aspire to. Show me how to speak life to others in a way that points them to You. Fill me with a passion for Your kingdom. Pour into me to overflowing so that I have no choice but to overflow with Your life-giving Spirit into the lives of others. Speak to me. Guide me. I want to be used for Your glory. May all I do bring You pleasure all the days of my life.

INVITE GOD INTO EVERY DETAIL

When I heard this, I sat down and wept. I mourned for days, fasting and praying before the God-of-Heaven. I said, "GOD, God-of-Heaven, the great and awesome God, loyal to his covenant and faithful to those who love him and obey his commands: Look at me, listen to me. Pay attention to this prayer of your servant that I'm praying day and night in intercession for your servants, the People of Israel, confessing the sins of the People of Israel. And I'm including myself, I and my ancestors, among those who have sinned against you." … "Well, there they are—your servants, your people whom you so powerfully and impressively redeemed. O Master, listen to me, listen to your servant's prayer—and yes, to all your servants who delight in honoring you—and make me successful today so that I get what I want from the king."

Nehemiah 1:4-6, 10-11 MSG

- Are you pursuing your passion? If not, what is keeping you from pursuing your dream?
- Have you invited God to participate as an equal partner in your pursuit?
- Do you need to start where Nehemiah started, by remembering who God is and what He's done in your life so far?
- Are there things you know shouldn't be in your life—bad habits you want to break, relationships that have tied you to the wrong crowd, or hidden hurts you can't seem to forgive?
- Do you need to confess some things to God?
- Do you want positive change in your life but realize you don't have the power to make those changes?
- Have you ever thought that God has bigger issues to deal with, and you didn't want to bother Him with yours? The truth is, what's important to you is also important to Him. Prayer opens the door to relationship, but you have to invite Him in!

God, You know my heart and the very passions that are deep within my soul. Honestly, I've not come to You about this much because I have my own ideas of how I want to see it play out. I want to control the outcome. Forgive me for not believing that Your plan for me is even better than I could ever dream.

The path I've chosen is often my own, but today I invite You to lead this journey. Show me the course corrections I need to make that will bring me to the destination You have purposed for my life. I ask You to reach deep within the well of my heart and bring up the dream. Show it to me in the light of Your love. Let me see my dream anew from Your perspective. Thank You for joining me on this journey.

HIGHLY FAVORED

‖‖‖

And Esther found favor in the sight of all who saw her. So Esther was taken to King Ahasuerus, to his royal palace in the tenth month, that is, the month of Tebeth (Dec-Jan), in the seventh year of his reign. Now the king loved Esther more than all the other women, and she found favor and kindness with him more than all the [other] virgins, so that he set the royal crown on her head and made her queen in the place of Vashti. Then the king held a great banquet, Esther's banquet, for all his officials and his servants; and he made a festival for the provinces and gave gifts in accordance with the resources of the king.

ESTHER 2:15–18 AMP

‖‖‖

- The Lord blessed Esther with favor in the eyes of everyone who saw her. Have you ever been the favorite? If not, have you ever wished you were?

- God used Esther to save the lives of her people—to turn man's deathly plan around for her people's good. When has God turned a difficulty into a blessing in your life? Have you seen a bad situation suddenly turn out for good?

- God's favor can bring blessing into every area of your life. When have you experienced God's favor in your life?

- When have you found yourself in the right place at the right time for things to work out in your favor? Did you see it as happenstance, or did you recognize it as God's favor?

- Have you ever felt like you missed God's favor? Why or why not?

- Esther listened to wisdom from godly mentors in her life, and as a result she experienced God's favor. Do you have godly mentors and teachers? If not, ask God to bring those relationships into your life.

*Heavenly Father, I am Your child, and
therefore I am blessed. You want to pour out
Your favor on me. Forgive me for the times
You've prepared blessing and I got in the way.
Forgive me for trying to make things happen
all by myself—in my timing instead of Yours.
Give me ears to hear wisdom when You speak.
I will listen to those You've placed in my life
to mentor me and guide me. I will recognize
Your wisdom when You call me. I choose to be
pliable and moldable. I don't want to be stiff
and inflexible to Your will. I choose Your way
and not my own. My plans are big, but in no
way do they compare to Yours. You saved
my life. May Your favor rest on me
all the days of my life.*

FAITHFUL ASSURANCE

,,,

*And by this we know that we are of the truth, and shall
assure our hearts before Him. For if our heart condemns us,
God is greater than our heart, and knows all things. Beloved,
if our heart does not condemn us, we have confidence toward
God. And whatever we ask we receive from Him, because we
keep His commandments and do those things that are pleasing
in His sight. And this is His commandment: that we should
believe on the name of His Son Jesus Christ and love
one another, as He gave us commandment.*

1 JOHN 3:19–23 NKJV

,,,

- Have you ever had thoughts that caused you to question your salvation?

- It's easy to focus on the wrong things as proof that your salvation is real. Have you ever considered God's work in your life, spiritual growth, or your good works as proof of your salvation?

- Those things are evidence of your faith walk, but they don't give you assurance of your salvation. Your salvation is assured the moment you accept Christ. Have you accepted His gift?

- How can you better understand that God's gift of salvation requires nothing more than simple acceptance?

- There's nothing you can do to earn God's gift. What does it mean to you to know your salvation comes with no strings attached?

*Heavenly Father, thank You for my salvation.
It is a gift—something I could never work for
to get, but a treasure given freely with no
strings attached. It is mine and I receive it.
It can never be taken from me. Your Word
says that nothing can separate me from Your
love. Forgive me for the times that I doubted
my salvation or mistakenly believed it was
something I need to achieve or win. Thank
You for believing in me, trusting me with Your
love. I can rest knowing that You accept me
just the way I am. Help me to hear Your voice.
Show me how to discern between guilt and
conviction. I can stand in confidence each
day knowing I am saved and I belong to You.
My salvation is assured. May I live each day
with a growing desire to live my life according
to Your purpose. I want to please You in all I
do. Give me strength to choose You each day.*

BOLDLY STAND IN FAITH

||||||||||||||||||||||||||||||||||||||||||||||||||||||||||||||||||||||||||||

Brothers and sisters, you are holy partners in a heavenly calling.
So look carefully at Jesus. . . Jesus is faithful to God. . .in the same
way that Moses was faithful when he served in God's house.
Jesus deserves more praise than Moses in the same way that
the builder of a house is praised more than the house. After all,
every house has a builder, but the builder of everything is God.
Moses was a faithful servant in God's household. He told the
people what God would say in the future. But Christ is a
faithful son in charge of God's household. We are his
household if we continue to have courage and to
be proud of the confidence we have.

HEBREWS 3:1–6 GW

||||||||||||||||||||||||||||||||||||||||||||||||||||||||||||||||||||||||||||

- It's natural to avoid danger. Do you normally want to walk away from conflict?
- Do you choose comfort and ease over sacrifice and pain?
- Have you found yourself to be more courageous knowing Christ lives in you?
- When have you stood firm in Christ when you really wanted to run away?
- Why did you take a stand?
- Who did you take the stand for? Yourself? A friend or family member? Christ?
- Does your courage and hope make your faith real to you? Why?
- When the winds of life's circumstances blow, how does your confidence in Christ stabilize you and help you to hold on to the courage to stand firm?
- In what areas of your life are you the most courageous with your faith?
- In what areas do you need more courage?

Jesus, thank You for making a way for me to know You and for Your Spirit to live in me. When I think I can't step up and stand firm in the face of adversity, You give me courage and hope. My confidence in Your faithfulness gives me what I need to take my stand. I firmly plant my feet in hope and am committed to endure because I have faith in You. You will uphold me. You always protect me and keep me. When I'm tempted to give up, You whisper Your words of hope and truth. You remind me that I am Yours and You are mine. I belong to You. You are my faithful and steady anchor. Whatever situation is before me, I can win because You give me the victory. In You I am more than a conqueror.

GENEROUSLY SUPPLIED

||||||||||||||||||||||||||||||||||||||||||||||||||||||||||||||||||||||||

But remember this—if you give little, you will get little. A farmer who plants just a few seeds will get only a small crop, but if he plants much, he will reap much. Everyone must make up his own mind as to how much he should give. Don't force anyone to give more than he really wants to, for cheerful givers are the ones God prizes. God is able to make it up to you by giving you everything you need and more so that there will not only be enough for your own needs but plenty left over to give joyfully to others. It is as the Scriptures say: "The godly man gives generously to the poor. His good deeds will be an honor to him forever." For God, who gives seed to the farmer to plant, and later on good crops to harvest and eat, will give you more and more seed to plant and will make it grow so that you can give away more and more fruit from your harvest.

2 Corinthians 9:6–10 TLB

||||||||||||||||||||||||||||||||||||||||||||||||||||||||||||||||||||||||

- When it comes to the things you have, do you grip them tightly or hold them loosely?
- God told Abraham that He would bless him so that he could become a blessing to others, even into future generations. Do you believe you are blessed to be a blessing?
- Do you consider yourself a generous person?
- Sometimes having very little growing up or suffering financial loss can cause you to hold on to every increase you receive. Do you have some past experience that compels you to hold tight to money or the things you have?
- Would you say that everything you have belongs to God? Why or why not?
- Do you consider God generous?
- Are you expecting a harvest from the good seeds you have sown in your life?

God, You are a generous giver. Your Word says You will provide seed to the sower and in due season I will reap a harvest. Thank You for the seed I've sown and for the harvest that is on the way. Forgive me where I've missed the mark in financial decisions. Open my eyes to any opportunity I may have missed to receive from You. Thank You that everything I put my hand to is blessed and brings blessing into my life. Thank You for each opportunity to be generous to others. Show me where You would have me give into the lives of others. Lord, You know what I need. You know the situation I'm facing financially. I receive Your wisdom in order to receive and be abundantly supplied. You meet my every need in Jesus' name.

JESUS, THE ROCK AT THE BOTTOM

As you come to him, the living Stone—rejected by humans but chosen by God and precious to him—you also, like living stones, are being built into a spiritual house to be a holy priesthood, offering spiritual sacrifices acceptable to God through Jesus Christ. For in Scripture it says: "See, I lay a stone in Zion, a chosen and precious cornerstone, and the one who trusts in him will never be put to shame." Now to you who believe, this stone is precious. But to those who do not believe, "The stone the builders rejected has become the cornerstone," and, "A stone that causes people to stumble and a rock that makes them fall." They stumble because they disobey the message—which is also what they were destined for.

1 PETER 2:4–8 NIV

- Throughout scripture God and Jesus are referred to as "the rock of your salvation." What emotions does that expression evoke in you? What images does the phrase bring to your mind?

- How many times have you reached rock bottom only to find Jesus right there, the rock at the bottom?

- What does it mean to you to have a trustworthy, rock-solid Savior?

- Have you told God what it meant to you to find Him at your lowest point?

- When you're tempted to have a pity party or get down on yourself, how does the image of Jesus as your rock change your perspective?

- What areas of your life feel unstable right now?

- How does your relationship with the Rock bring balance and stability into your world?

- What things are you holding on to that you need to let go of in order to gain a better grasp of Jesus?

Jesus, You are the rock of my salvation.
You are the one I hang on to through the
violent maelstroms life brings. When I can't
trust others—and forget how to trust myself—
I remember that You are the One I can always
depend on. You are faithful to show me the
way up, even when the sky is so dark I can't
see it. When I am broken and feel alone,
You are there. When I feel my life spinning
out of control, You settle my mind as I try to
fix my thoughts on You. When I experience
success and have much to celebrate, You are
there. You are my strength, my stability,
my strong tower. Thank You, Jesus!
Thank You for being a constant,
faithful friend. Thank You for bringing
wisdom and truth into my life.
You anchor my soul.

O MY SOUL, JUST LET GO

As a deer longs for flowing streams, so my soul longs for you, O God. My soul thirsts for God, for the living God. When may I come to see God's face? My tears are my food day and night. People ask me all day long, "Where is your God?" I will remember these things as I pour out my soul: how I used to walk with the crowd and lead it in a procession to God's house. I sang songs of joy and thanksgiving while crowds of people celebrated a festival. Why are you discouraged, my soul? Why are you so restless? Put your hope in God, because I will still praise him. He is my savior and my God.

Psalm 42:1–5 gw

- When you experience grief, hurt, pain, or loss, where do you turn?
- Do you isolate yourself? Why?
- Why do our souls hold on to the hurt, the disappointment, and the grief?
- Do you find it hard to let go?
- When you're at a loss for answers about the deep disappointments in life, is it hard to trust God? Why?
- When you can't help but think of the hurt, how do you turn your heart and mind to the Lord?
- What past experiences of God's love encourage you to push forward and reach out to Him now?
- What actions can you take to help you let go of the pain?
- What things do you want to say to God, but are afraid to say or feel guilty in admitting? Can you say those things to Him now?

*God, I want the pain to go away. I'm hurt,
angry, and disappointed. Why did this
happen? Why didn't You stop it? What should
I be learning here? What am I missing?
What is my grief blinding me from seeing?
I want to let go—to forgive—to forget in
some way. I want to have peace in my soul.
Help me to take all the emotions I'm feeling
and share them with You. I don't understand,
but You do. You can show me another way to
look at this picture. Only You can heal what
is broken and make me new. How can I help
others in this situation, or one similar?
Let my thoughts become Your thoughts.
I let go and give it all to You, now.*

GOD'S WILL FOR YOU

"Here's what I want you to do: Find a quiet, secluded place so you won't be tempted to role-play before God. Just be there as simply and honestly as you can manage. The focus will shift from you to God, and you will begin to sense his grace. The world is full of so-called prayer warriors who are prayer-ignorant. They're full of formulas and programs and advice, peddling techniques for getting what you want from God. Don't fall for that nonsense. This is your Father you are dealing with, and he knows better than you what you need. With a God like this loving you, you can pray very simply. Like this: Our Father in heaven, reveal who you are. Set the world right; do what's best—as above, so below. Keep us alive with three square meals. Keep us forgiven with you and forgiving others. Keep us safe from ourselves and the Devil. You're in charge! You can do anything you want! You're ablaze in beauty! Yes. Yes. Yes."

MATTHEW 6:6–13 MSG

- Very few people hear God's voice audibly. He leads you in different ways. How does God speak to you?
- What decisions do you have before you right now?
- Have you asked God about His desire and plan regarding that decision?
- Do you feel like you understand the direction God wants you to go?
- What does it mean for you to have peace concerning a decision?
- Does the direction you're leaning in line up with God's Word?
- Have you spoken with a Christian mentor or friend?
- Have you taken some time to examine your own motives? Can you truthfully say you are choosing God's will and not your own?

Lord, I know You have a plan for my life. Before I was born, You established my purpose. I want to know You and recognize Your voice. I want to live my life in agreement with Your will. I will listen to Your wisdom.

Wisdom cries out to me and says to me, "This is the way, walk in it." I hear Your voice and will do as You ask. Give me ears to hear what Your Spirit is speaking to me. Alert me to danger and keep my steps steady. Even if the way I should go seems hard, give me peace to know I am following You. Examine my heart, Lord, and reveal to me any selfish motives that I may have. Sometimes I find myself going my own way. Put a stop sign in my path when I've inadvertently gone my own way. I choose to do things Your way and in Your time. Give me patience and persistence as I seek Your ways.

HELP FROM HEAVEN

*"Anyone who does not love me will not obey my teaching.
These words you hear are not my own; they belong to the
Father who sent me. All this I have spoken while still with you.
But the Advocate, the Holy Spirit, whom the Father will send
in my name, will teach you all things and will remind you of
everything I have said to you. Peace I leave with you; my peace
I give you. I do not give to you as the world gives. Do not let
your hearts be troubled and do not be afraid. You heard me
say, 'I am going away and I am coming back to you.' If you
loved me, you would be glad that I am going to the Father,
for the Father is greater than I. I have told you now before it
happens, so that when it does happen you will believe."*

JOHN 14:24–29 NIV

- Jesus promised help from heaven for all who follow Him. Have you ever felt alone?
- When have you felt pressure to fix things in your life on your own?
- When was your aha moment that revealed God was available to you?
- What does it mean to you to know that the Father sent you someone to walk with you?
- Have you ever felt the Holy Spirit whispering encouragement or words of wisdom along the way?
- When have you been afraid and the Holy Spirit offered comfort and assurance?
- How does the Holy Spirit help you deal with anxiety?
- How have you responded to the Holy Spirit's presence?

Jesus, thank You for making the Holy Spirit known to me. I am grateful to the Father for sending me His help. Sometimes I forget that I don't have to work things out on my own. I don't have to have the answers. That's why You have sent the Holy Spirit. I believe He stands next to me. He advocates for me. He speaks wisdom to me and teaches me all things. Because He is always with me, I will not be afraid. I will not allow anxiety to consume me. I will hold fast to the truth of His presence in my life. I accept His comfort and assurance when I feel unsteady. Today I am determined to access the help from heaven that has been given to me. Whatever difficulties are before me, I can make it because I don't walk alone.

ASKING THE RIGHT QUESTIONS

,,,

*For when the way is rough, your patience has a chance to grow.
So let it grow, and don't try to squirm out of your problems. For
when your patience is finally in full bloom, then you will
be ready for anything, strong in character, full and complete.
If you want to know what God wants you to do, ask him, and
he will gladly tell you, for he is always ready to give a bountiful
supply of wisdom to all who ask him; he will not resent it.
But when you ask him, be sure that you really expect him to
tell you, for a doubtful mind will be as unsettled as a wave
of the sea that is driven and tossed by the wind; and every
decision you then make will be uncertain, as you turn first
this way and then that. If you don't ask with faith,
don't expect the Lord to give you any solid answer.*

JAMES 1:3–8 TLB

,,,

- What decisions are you facing today?
- Asking the right questions is important to discovering God's best for your life. So, what question or questions do you need to ask today?
- What are you asking God to reveal to you? What decision are you leaning toward that brings peace to your heart?
- What perspective are you missing? Ask God to show you His perspective.
- Do you feel like you're in the midst of a trial?
- How can you grow in your faith as you make this decision?
- How do you feel about God's promises to give you His wisdom?
- What adjustments do you need to make to your thinking in order to truly believe God will give you a solid answer?

Lord, You know the decision I am facing today. You know my heart and my desire to please You more than anything else. It's human nature for me to ask why—why I'm faced with this—but I know there are better questions to ask. Help me to discover the right questions to ask of You in order to see Your wisdom and realize the answers You have for me. Help me not to be afraid of the answer, because only Your best can come from this. You lead me in the way I should go. Please show me how You look at this situation. Give me eyes to see things from the right perspective. Help me to learn and grow in my faith as I navigate this decision. Help me to adjust any thinking I have that is contrary to Your Word. I trust You will give me the answers I need in such a way that I understand clearly the next step I need to take. Thank You for Your peace.

WITH APPRECIATION

''

*I thank my God in every remembrance of you, always offering
every prayer of mine with joy [and with specific requests] for all
of you.... And this I pray, that your love may abound more and
more [displaying itself in greater depth] in real knowledge and in
practical insight, so that you may learn to recognize and treasure
what is excellent [identifying the best, and distinguishing moral
differences], and that you may be pure and blameless until the
day of Christ [actually living lives that lead others away from sin];
filled with the fruit of righteousness which comes through
Jesus Christ, to the glory and praise of God [so that His
glory may be both revealed and recognized].*

PHILIPPIANS 1:3–4, 9–11 AMP

''

- Who comes to mind when you read Paul's prayer for the Philippians?
- In addition to your relationship with God, what relationships are you thankful to Him for in your life?
- What would your life look like without these people?
- What about them makes them special to you?
- How do you feel when you're around them?
- Do they feel the same about you?
- What do they add to your life? What do you add to their lives?
- Would you consider any of them a mentor?
- How important is mentorship to you?
- Do you know that God has specifically placed them in your life? What is their purpose? What is your purpose in their lives?
- How can you show them how much you appreciate them?

God, thank You for the relationships You've placed in my life. Thank You for the people who push me to be more like You. I appreciate their encouragement, strength, love, and honesty. Even though I don't like it at times, I need their candid comments about the choices I make. I need them to call me out when I'm not giving my best or doing what I need to fulfill my God-given purpose. I know they love me unconditionally, no matter what I do or say. I know that is You loving me through them too. I pray for them right now, Lord. You know what they need. You know the struggles they may never share with me. Help me to be a good friend and to love them unconditionally. Show me how I can demonstrate Your love through the words I say and by the actions I take. Thank You for the special connection in our hearts that makes us good for one another.

MIRACLES FROM EVEN
THE SMALLEST THINGS

IIIIIIIIIIIIIIIIIIIIIIIIIIIIIIIIIIIIIIIIIIIIIIIIIIIIIIIIIIIIIIIIIIIIIIII

*Elijah said to Ahab, "Go up, eat and drink; for there is the sound
of abundance of rain." So Ahab went up to eat and drink.
And Elijah went up to the top of Carmel; then he bowed down
on the ground. . .and said to his servant, "Go up now, look toward
the sea." So he went up and looked, and said, "There is nothing."
And seven times he said, "Go again." . . . The seventh time, he said,
"There is a cloud, as small as a man's hand, rising out of the sea!"
So he said, "Go up, say to Ahab, 'Prepare your chariot, and go
down before the rain stops you.'" . . .in the meantime the sky
became black with clouds and wind, and there was a heavy rain.
So Ahab rode away and went to Jezreel. Then the hand of the
LORD came upon Elijah; and he girded up his loins
and ran ahead of Ahab to the entrance of Jezreel.*

1 KINGS 18:41–46 NKJV

IIIIIIIIIIIIIIIIIIIIIIIIIIIIIIIIIIIIIIIIIIIIIIIIIIIIIIIIIIIIIIIIIIIIIIII

- After three years of drought and not a sign of rain in the sky, Elijah said he heard the sound of abundant rain. His servant couldn't see anything until his seventh trip to look for the rain, and even then it was a cloud the size of a man's fist. When have you believed when no one else could see something God promised you?

- Elijah's rainstorm was only a small cloud at first. What seed of faith have you given God to work with lately?

- What do you believe God wants to do in your life?

- What hope are you holding on to?

- What do you see by faith—even if it's only something small in the distance?

- Do you believe in miracles?

- What miracles has God performed in your life? And do you share those stories of His faithfulness with others?

*Heavenly Father, thank You for doing
the miraculous in my heart and in my life.
Forgive me when I've doubted, and help me
to trust You more each day. When You speak
to me and give me a promise, I will hold fast
to it. I will believe You and encourage myself
in Your Word. Even when it looks like the
smallest thing—such as a cloud the size of
a man's fist—I will stand strong and see the
abundant rain poured out lavishly on my life.
Your Word says we all have a measure of
faith given to us. I will use my faith today to
stand firm and to believe You will faithfully
complete the work that You've begun in me.*

CHOOSING TO FOLLOW GOD'S LEAD

‚‚

And when [Ruth] went back to work again, Boaz told his young men to let her glean right among the sheaves without stopping her, and to snap off some heads of barley and drop them on purpose for her to glean, and not to make any remarks. So she worked there all day, and in the evening when she had beaten out the barley she had gleaned, it came to a whole bushel! She carried it back into the city and gave it to her mother-in-law, with what was left of her lunch. "So much!" Naomi exclaimed. "Where in the world did you glean today? Praise the Lord for whoever was so kind to you." So Ruth told her mother-in-law all about it and mentioned that the owner of the field was Boaz. "Praise the Lord for a man like that! God has continued his kindness to us as well as to your dead husband!" Naomi cried excitedly. "Why, that man is one of our closest relatives!"

RUTH 2:15–20 TLB

‚‚

- It's easy to make plans and expect God to bless them, but how often do you ask for His will for your life?

- Do you truly want to fulfill God's purpose for your life?

- Do you worry that you won't like the direction God takes your life if you give Him permission to lead?

- Have you ever refused to follow the Holy Spirit's promptings in your heart? How did that turn out?

- How do you seek God's guidance?

- When circumstances "just happen" or seem like a coincidence, do you stop to think that perhaps God is ordering your steps?

- Has God brought things together in your life in such a way that you knew it had to be God? When?

*You are God and I am not. Help me to
remember that You know me and that
You have placed me on this earth with a
divine purpose. I want to fulfill that purpose.
Thank You, God, for the many times I chose my
own way and You still blessed me. I appreciate
the times You reached down and corrected my
course. I give You permission to lead my life
today. Whatever dream I have, Your plans are
higher. Forgive me when I forget that. Give me
ears to hear Your voice and a heart that desires
to please You more than anything else. I don't
want to follow my own road; I choose to walk
in the path You've set before me.*

OVERCOMING BETRAYAL

,,

This isn't the neighborhood bully mocking me—I could take
that. This isn't a foreign devil spitting invective—I could tune
that out. It's you! We grew up together! You! My best friend!
Those long hours of leisure as we walked arm in arm, God a
third party to our conversation. Haul my betrayers off alive
to hell—let them experience the horror, let them feel every
desolate detail of a damned life. I call to God; GOD will help
me. At dusk, dawn, and noon I sigh deep sighs—he hears,
he rescues. My life is well and whole, secure in the middle
of danger even while thousands are lined up against me.
God hears it all, and from his judge's bench
puts them in their place.

PSALM 55:12-19 MSG

,,

- Everyone experiences pain. David's own son, Absalom, betrayed him, and he wasn't the first one. Who has hurt you, even betrayed you?

- What emotions are you feeling? What actions do you want to take?

- Jesus also experienced the betrayal of a close friend and ultimately forgave him. Is that something you're willing to do too?

- Have you tried to overcome the betrayal on your own? If you haven't asked Jesus to help you, why not?

- Do you find it difficult to forgive and ask for help? Could it be because you're holding tight to the offense?

- Is your desire for that person to experience the same emotions you're feeling more important than reconciling your heart to peace and to God?

- What will it take for you to let go?

- Do you know what you need to do to be free from the pain?

Jesus, I'm hurt! I'm angry. I can't believe I opened my heart and became vulnerable to this person, only to have them betray me like this. Maybe I do want to see them hurt. Maybe I do feel like they owe me something for this injustice. If I let go of this offense and forgive, it feels like I'm condoning what they did. And that's not true. The reality is I must forgive them or this pain will imprison me for the rest of my life. It won't go away. Please help me choose to forgive. I can't do it on my own. It has to be something I do by faith. So, I give it to You, Jesus. I release it all to You. I will not harbor ill will toward them, but I won't put myself in a position to be hurt again either. I say goodbye to the pain and the relationship I once shared with them. It's going to be awkward, but I can now have peace.

IN A CHILD'S EYES

*Children are a heritage from the LORD, offspring a reward from
him. Like arrows in the hands of a warrior are children born
in one's youth. Blessed is the man whose quiver is full of them.
They will not be put to shame when they contend with their
opponents in court. . . . Start children off on the way they should
go, and even when they are old they will not turn from it.*

PSALM 127:3-5; PROVERBS 22:6 NIV

- All believers, whether they have children or not, have a responsibility to live their lives in such a way that those who see them can follow their example and come to know God. Do you have children of your own? If not, what children has God placed in your life?
- What blessings have you bestowed on a child lately—praise, encouragement, demonstrations of God's goodness or love?
- When was the last time you took time to really listen to a child? What did he or she say?
- What have you learned about God from a child?
- What have you learned about yourself because of your relationship with a child?
- What do children see when they look at you?
- Do children have any expectations of you?
- What melts your heart?
- What makes you angry?
- Have there been times when you chose to be too busy for a child? Once you realized you'd done that, how did it make you feel? What about the child?
- What can you do differently that will improve your relationship with them?

Heavenly Father, thank You for the precious children You've placed in my life. Life is busy, and I have been preoccupied at times. Remind me that little eyes are watching, taking in all I do. They see me on my good days and my tough ones. When I make a mistake in front of them, or even with them, stop me and show me how to wisely set things right. Teach me to be humble enough and vulnerable enough to ask them to forgive me as I admit to them when I've been wrong. Give me a heart to see them as You do. Each child is individually called by You for the purpose You have for their life. Give me wisdom to recognize their gifts and talents and draw those gifts out. May they grow up knowing and serving You all the days of their lives. May my life be a witness to them to become all You have called them to be.

ON THE SAME TEAM

⁣

I beg you—I, a prisoner here in jail for serving the Lord—to live and act in a way worthy of those who have been chosen for such wonderful blessings as these. Be humble and gentle. Be patient with each other, making allowance for each other's faults because of your love. Try always to be led along together by the Holy Spirit and so be at peace with one another. We are all parts of one body, we have the same Spirit, and we have all been called to the same glorious future. For us there is only one Lord, one faith, one baptism, and we all have the same God and Father who is over us all and in us all, and living through every part of us. However, Christ has given each of us special abilities—whatever he wants us to have out of his rich storehouse of gifts.

EPHESIANS 4:1-7 TLB

⁣

- Marriage is work, and it takes two people doing the work. If you're married, do you pray together?
- How do you make the Lord the center of your relationship?
- During any crisis, it's easy to turn your attention to what went wrong and why it's wrong and to point fingers at the person you blame. Do you find yourself in a crisis of marriage today?
- What do you think divides the two of you?
- The enemy wants to divide and destroy your marriage. Do you ever feel like you give him ammunition?
- What is good in your marriage?
- What made you believe you should get married in the first place?
- What do you love most about your spouse? Have you shared that with them?

*God, thank You for my spouse. Thank You
for my marriage. Teach us to pray together.
Give us eyes to see each other with Your love
for us. Forgive me when I've not been a team
player. Help me to see when I am selfish and
self-serving. Help me to put my spouse first,
after my relationship with You. Help us to
work together and play together. Build our
trust in one another as each day we become
a stronger team. I am on my spouse's side.
I am my spouse's biggest fan. Help me to
share my love and appreciation. Help me
to acknowledge even the smallest act of
kindness. I will choose my words wisely. I will
be careful not to offend but to speak the truth
in love. May all I do and say, especially when
it comes to my spouse, be pleasing in Your
sight. Knit our hearts together and cause
us to truly become one heart for You.*

NEW EMPLOYMENT

,,

*Go your way, eat your bread with joy and drink your wine with
a cheerful heart [if you are righteous, wise, and in the hands of
God]; for God has already approved and accepted your works.
Let your clothes always be white [with purity], and do not let the oil
[of gladness] be lacking on your head. Live joyfully with the wife
whom you love all the days of your fleeting life which He has given
you under the sun—all the days of vanity and futility. For this is your
reward in life and in your work in which you have labored under
the sun. Whatever your hand finds to do, do it with all your might;
for there is no activity or planning or knowledge or wisdom in Sheol
(the nether world, the place of the dead) where you are going.*

ECCLESIASTES 9:7–10 AMP

,,

- God promises to provide for those who have given themselves to Him. Have you placed yourself in His care?
- A lack of finances affects every area of your life. How does your financial situation impact you today?
- How do you feel emotionally, physically, spiritually?
- Do you have any regrets you need to take to the Lord concerning your current situation?
- Do you need to ask Him or anyone for forgiveness?
- Financial loss can sometimes occur unjustly. Do you have unresolved emotions toward past employers or coworkers that need to be resolved?
- Have you taken these feelings and thoughts to God in prayer?
- Your mind, will, and emotions are on high alert. What do you do to maintain your peace when facing financial difficulty?
- What promises in God's Word encourage you to trust Him to provide for you? For your family?

Heavenly Father, You are my peace in the midst of financial crisis. Forgive me, Lord, for anything I've done to contribute to this situation. When I feel unjustly set aside by a former employer, help me to let go of those feelings. Help me to forgive. I know that when my heart is fixed on You, I am able to do all things through Christ who gives me strength. You have a plan for the next job. You are already positioning me with favor in the eyes of the decision maker. I trust You to place me in a good job. You will turn this situation for my good. You will make a way for me. My ears are open to hear from heaven concerning the right job for me. Give me peace and patience. Settle my heart and stabilize my emotions. Increase my faith and help me to believe that the best is yet to come.

THE DOORKEEPER

" 'He who has an ear, let him hear what the Spirit says to the churches.' And to the angel of the church in Philadelphia write, 'These things says He who is holy, He who is true, "He who has the key of David, He who opens and no one shuts, and shuts and no one opens": "I know your works. See, I have set before you an open door, and no one can shut it; for you have a little strength, have kept My word, and have not denied My name. . . . Behold, I am coming quickly! Hold fast what you have, that no one may take your crown. He who overcomes, I will make him a pillar in the temple of My God, and he shall go out no more. I will write on him the name of My God and the name of the city of My God, the New Jerusalem, which comes down out of heaven from My God. And I will write on him My new name." ' "

REVELATION 3:6–8, 11–12 NKJV

- Jesus is speaking of open doors to eternal life, but He also is the doorkeeper for your life. Do you find discerning His direction for your life difficult sometimes?
- God opens doors no man can shut and shuts doors no man can open. What doors has He opened for you in your life?
- What did you learn about yourself as you crossed the threshold into that next season?
- Did you ever refuse to enter a door God opened?
- When have you struggled to stay on the path because you lacked patience to wait for God to open the door? What did you learn?
- What rewards has patience produced in your past?
- Have you asked God to open specific doors for you?
- God's direction can be clear if you ask Him specifically to show you the way He would have you go. Have you asked?

58

*Jesus, thank You for Your specific direction
for my life. I want to follow You in all Your
ways. I want to know I am walking in the
path You've set before me. When I come to a
choice of many doors, show me the way to go.
Speak to my heart and direct me through the
open door. Give me Your wisdom to discern
the truth of my circumstances. I will not be
deceived. I will not miss the mark. Forgive
me, Lord, when I refused to go through the
door You had opened for me. Give me that
opportunity again to travel that road. Lord,
open the doors that are Your perfect will.
Thank You for making it clear to me.
You are my doorkeeper.*

NEVER WITHOUT HOPE

,,

In every way we're troubled, but we aren't crushed by our troubles. We're frustrated, but we don't give up. We're persecuted, but we're not abandoned. We're captured, but we're not killed. We always carry around the death of Jesus in our bodies so that the life of Jesus is also shown in our bodies. While we are alive, we are constantly handed over to death for Jesus' sake so that the life of Jesus is also shown in our mortal nature. Death is at work in us, but life is at work in you. The following is written, "I believed; therefore, I spoke." We have that same spirit of faith. We also believe; therefore, we also speak. We know that the one who brought the Lord Jesus back to life will also bring us back to life through Jesus. He will present us to God together with you.

2 Corinthians 4:8–14 GW

,,

- Have you ever felt excruciating pressure from circumstances to the point that you thought there just might not be a way out?
- In those moments, what were you most focused on?
- Jesus said this world is full of trouble, but you have biblical hope, which is a reality and not a feeling. What did it take for you to rediscover your hope in Christ? Did God use a person to encourage you, the Bible to speak to you, or something else to put your eyes back on Him?
- What does it mean to you to recognize that no matter how bad it gets, you are never without confidence and assurance that God will get you through?
- How do you inspire hope in others?

*Lord, You are my hope. I take my eyes
off my circumstances and look to You.
No matter how loud the circumstances shout,
I turn my attention to You. When my heart
is overwhelmed and I throw my hands up
without answers, my hope rests on eternity.
Just as the psalmist shared his deepest
feelings in the words he wrote, I open my
heart to You and share what I'm feeling.
In the end, I am nothing without You. You will
never leave me nor forsake me. I am never
without hope. I turn my thoughts to the
many wonderful blessings You've given
and the miracles You've done on my behalf.
This situation will be no different. You are at
work on my behalf, bringing out Your good
in my life. I am confident You will bring me
through this. I will stand on the other side
and praise You for all You've done. I will tell
others of Your love and encourage
them in the hope of my salvation.*

TURNING DOWN THE NOISE

*In Jerusalem at the time, there was a man, Simeon by name,
a good man, a man who lived in the prayerful expectancy of
help for Israel. And the Holy Spirit was on him. The Holy Spirit
had shown him that he would see the Messiah of God before he
died. Led by the Spirit, he entered the Temple. As the parents
of the child Jesus brought him in to carry out the rituals of the
Law, Simeon took him into his arms and blessed God. . . . Anna
the prophetess was also there, a daughter of Phanuel from
the tribe of Asher. She was by now a very old woman. She had
been married seven years and a widow for eighty-four.
She never left the Temple area, worshiping night and day
with her fastings and prayers. At the very time Simeon
was praying, she showed up, broke into an anthem of
praise to God, and talked about the child to all who were
waiting expectantly for the freeing of Jerusalem.*

LUKE 2:25–28, 36–38 MSG

- Would you say that life is too loud sometimes?
- Do you ever struggle to hear God?
- What things can distract you from tuning in to God? List them.
- A fast is a time when you determine to remove yourself from specific distractions. Have you ever fasted?
- Besides food, what "noises" in your life need to be turned down so you can hear what God is saying to you?
- What do you believe a fast can do for you?
- Is God calling you to a fast? What does that look like for you?
- What is God asking you to give up in order to hear Him more clearly?

Heavenly Father, the volume of life is overwhelming sometimes. I don't know exactly how to turn down the noise or block it out. I want to hear You, but I allow distraction. Fasting and prayer are important. They go hand in hand. Are You calling me to a season of fasting? What does that look like for me? What things would You have me let go of? What habits do I need to change so that I can hear You better? Lead me and guide me, even in the smallest things. I don't want to miss a single opportunity to please You. I have to be tuned in to You so that I can be used by You in the lives of others. Today I am ready, willing, and open to give up some things so that I can totally focus on You. Please show me how.

THE ANSWER IS LOVE

"You have heard that it was said, 'Love your neighbor and hate your enemy.' But I tell you, love your enemies and pray for those who persecute you, that you may be children of your Father in heaven. He causes his sun to rise on the evil and the good, and sends rain on the righteous and the unrighteous. If you love those who love you, what reward will you get? Are not even the tax collectors doing that? And if you greet only your own people, what are you doing more than others? Do not even pagans do that? Be perfect, therefore, as your heavenly Father is perfect."

MATTHEW 5:43–48 NIV

- What's the biggest challenge you're facing today?
- Is it a person—what they did to you or said to you? Did they hurt someone you love?
- Do you find some relationships more difficult than others?
- Are you holding a grudge?
- Have you tried to let it go? Why or why not?
- While it's easy to get caught up in the drama and respond negatively, your heavenly Father wants you to respond with love. What is difficult about showing love to this particular person?
- Have you talked to your heavenly Father about it?
- Are you afraid you're not going to like what God has to say?

*Heavenly Father, relationships are hard.
People can be difficult. You know why it's
hard for me to respond with love, grace, and
forgiveness, especially in this situation. I want
to see this person pay for what they've done,
but that's not Your way. And that shouldn't be
my way either. There is a storm raging within
me. I am hurt, angry, and offended. But You
are the calm in the middle of this storm. You
have poured out Your love on me. And so I ask
You to teach me to love like You do. It is only
Your love at work in me that will allow me to
respond to this person the way You desire me
to. So please go to work on my heart so that
I can truly allow You to love through me. I let
go of the pain and say goodbye to the wrongs
done to me. Not for them, but for You—and for
me. I've searched for the answers, and none
of my answers are good. Your answer must
become my answer, and that answer is love.*

NO EXCUSES! GET MOVING!

,,

And they turned against Moses, whining, "Have you brought us out here to die in the desert because there were not enough graves for us in Egypt? Why did you make us leave Egypt?" . . . But Moses told the people, "Don't be afraid. Just stand where you are and watch, and you will see the wonderful way the Lord will rescue you today. The Egyptians you are looking at—you will never see them again. The Lord will fight for you, and you won't need to lift a finger!" Then the Lord said to Moses, "Quit praying and get the people moving! Forward, march! Use your rod—hold it out over the water, and the sea will open up a path before you, and all the people of Israel shall walk through on dry ground!"

EXODUS 14:11, 13–16 TLB

,,

- After spending time in prayer and carefully listening to God, you received an answer. Have you ever received an answer that frightened you a little?

- Did God give you the what but not the how?

- God often asks us to step out in faith beyond what we can do on our own so that we must depend on Him to do the work. How has God asked you to step out of your comfort zone?

- Have you ever decided you didn't like God's answer, so you went back to praying?

- If you ever took a step back after God asked you to act, how did you feel? Were you afraid? Did you find yourself whining and complaining like the Israelites?

- In the scripture above, the Lord said, "Get moving." Is there action God is waiting for you to take?

- How has your inaction affected your relationship with God?

- Just as the Israelites had to step into the water, are you willing to step out and do that next thing God has asked?

*God, I realize You want me to walk by faith.
I find it hard to do this next thing without
the whole picture, but I choose to be obedient
to Your direction. Forgive me for whining
and complaining. Forgive me for looking to
others for information and wisdom when Your
instruction wasn't what I had hoped for.
Thank You for answering my prayers and
giving me direction. Your Word says You
make a way before me in the wilderness.
I will walk behind You and follow in Your
steps. I trust that whatever I need along
the way, You will provide. I will no longer
procrastinate. I set things in motion today.*

PRAYER PROMISES

IIIIIIIIIIIIIIIIIIIIIIIIIIIIIIIIIIIIIIIIIIIIIIIIIIIIIIIIIIIIIIIIIIIIIIIIIIIII

"A woman, when she is in labor, has pain because her time [to give birth] has come; but when she has given birth to the child, she no longer remembers the anguish because of her joy that a child has come into the world. So for now you are in grief; but I will see you again, and [then] your hearts will rejoice, and no one will take away from you your [great] joy. In that day you will not [need to] ask Me about anything. I assure you and most solemnly say to you, whatever you ask the Father in My name [as My representative], He will give you. Until now you have not asked [the Father] for anything in My name; but now ask and keep on asking and you will receive, so that your joy may be full and complete."

JOHN 16:21-24 AMP

IIIIIIIIIIIIIIIIIIIIIIIIIIIIIIIIIIIIIIIIIIIIIIIIIIIIIIIIIIIIIIIIIIIIIIIIIIIII

- Do you ever feel like God is too busy for you?
- Have you ever held on to things, trying to work them out on your own because you imagined God had bigger issues at hand?
- Do you think someone else deserves God's time more than you do?
- Is it hard to believe that God not only is able to take care of the little things that concern you but also really wants to do it?
- Where do those thoughts come from? What past experiences have given you that impression of God?
- Can you see God as a good father who wants to give you His very best? Why or why not?
- What things are you holding close to your heart today?
- Do you believe God wants to provide the answer or show you how to solve the problem?

God, You are a good father. I sometimes try to save You time and put a lot of energy into working things out. Remind me to ask You to help me, even with the little things. You are limitless. Not only are You unrestricted in what You can do for me, but You want to be involved in every area of my life. You know those things I've been holding tightly. I open my heart and my hands and give those things to You. I want You to be the answer. Your way is so much better than anything I can think of. I invite You to join me. Please help me. Let's do this together.

PAUSE AND PRAY

,,

*" 'I have chosen you and have not cast you away: fear not,
for I am with you; be not dismayed, for I am your God. I will
strengthen you, yes, I will help you, I will uphold you with My
righteous right hand.' Behold, all those who were incensed
against you shall be ashamed and disgraced; they shall be
as nothing, and those who strive with you shall perish. You
shall seek them and not find them—those who contended with
you. Those who war against you shall be as nothing, as a
nonexistent thing. For I, the LORD your God, will hold your
right hand, saying to you, 'Fear not, I will help you.' "*

ISAIAH 41:9-13 NKJV

,,

- What is your first thought when you find yourself in an unexpected and difficult situation?
- Do you scramble to figure it out on your own?
- Do you reach out to your friends or family for counsel?
- How long does it take for you to remember that God is the one constant in your life who has the answers you need?
- Is it hard for you to step back from the situation?
- What fears are pressing in on you?
- What does it take for you to hit the PAUSE button, settle your spirit, and pray?
- How do you feel when you finally reach out to God with your troubles?
- What does it mean to you to know that you can take a deep breath and talk to God directly about His promise to strengthen, help, and uphold you?

Lord, I need You. You know what is going through my mind right now. You know my fears, but I acknowledge them to You anyway.

Give me strength to step back from the situation as I pause and pray. Give me fresh eyes to see everything from a new vantage point. I don't have to figure it out on my own. You are my help. You have the answers I need. You know the circumstances better than I do. I give You my fear, anxiety, and worry today.

I will do my best to let go and trust You to work all these things out for my good. When I'm tempted to stress, I will think of You behind the scenes working on the details. You bring the answers; You provide a way when I can't see it. Right now, I take a deep breath and take in Your strength and peace. As I exhale, I let go of anxiety and concern. You've got this! I have nothing to fear. I am holding on to You.

CONVERSATIONS WITH GOD

,,,

I'm not ashamed of the Good News. It is God's power to save everyone who believes, Jews first and Greeks as well. God's approval is revealed in this Good News. This approval begins and ends with faith as Scripture says, "The person who has God's approval will live by faith." God's anger is revealed from heaven against every ungodly and immoral thing people do as they try to suppress the truth by their immoral living. What can be known about God is clear to them because he has made it clear to them. From the creation of the world, God's invisible qualities, his eternal power and divine nature, have been clearly observed in what he made. As a result, people have no excuse.

ROMANS 1:16–20 GW

,,,

- God reveals Himself to us throughout creation. When you step out into nature, do you feel close to God? Why or why not?

- What kind of God does nature reveal to you?

- When you look at the earth and how it works to make things grow, what does that say to you about God?

- What does the way in which the ocean and land meet say to you about God's ability to order your own life?

- As you look at how a forest or the sea provides for what lives within it, what does that tell you about God and His provision for you?

- Do quiet moments in nature stir your soul?

- Does a hike in the woods compel you to speak to God?

- What does God's creation tell you about Him and how He feels about you?

God of all creation, when I see all You have made, I am filled with wonder and awe. Your intelligence, might, and power are like no other. Even the most intricate of details in how You created my world reveals who You are to me. You are a God of order and planning. You care about the smallest of us. If You are able to command the sea to separate from the sand, You can order my life and plan my destiny. I love You and want to fulfill Your purpose. I want to become all You created me to be. You have provided for me and perfected those things that concern me. Help me to listen to Your wisdom and understand those things You want me to know. Fill me with understanding of who You are. Speak to me about my purpose, and reveal to me the path You've set before me.

THE FATHER'S FAVOR

||||||||||||||||||||||||||||||||||||||||||||||||||||||||||||||||||||||||||||

*My son, never forget the things I've taught you. If you want
a long and satisfying life, closely follow my instructions.
Never tire of loyalty and kindness. Hold these virtues tightly.
Write them deep within your heart. If you want favor with both
God and man, and a reputation for good judgment and common
sense, then trust the Lord completely; don't ever trust yourself.
In everything you do, put God first, and he will direct you and
crown your efforts with success. Don't be conceited, sure of
your own wisdom. Instead, trust and reverence the Lord,
and turn your back on evil; when you do that, then you will
be given renewed health and vitality. Honor the Lord by giving
him the first part of all your income, and he will fill your
barns with wheat and barley and overflow your
wine vats with the finest wines.*

PROVERBS 3:1–10 TLB

||||||||||||||||||||||||||||||||||||||||||||||||||||||||||||||||||||||||||||

- As Moses and Aaron went to Pharaoh with a message from God, their obedience produced more hardship for God's chosen people (Exodus 5:4–9). Sometimes adversity comes as a result of obedience to God, and it's easy to think you've fallen out of favor with Him. Have you ever experienced that?

- Even though on the outside it looked as if God had forgotten them, behind the scenes God was at work—eventually they saw freedom. When has God, unknowingly to you, been at work in your life?

- What are some small examples of how God has shown you His favor?

- When have you experienced God's favor in a big way?

- Do you always take time to thank God for His blessings in your life? How do you show Him your appreciation?

Heavenly Father, thank You for Your blessings
in my life. I take time right now to remember
some of those blessings. I never want to forget
the things You've taught me; I don't ever want
to overlook a single time when You've shown
me favor. I always will acknowledge that You
are at work in my life. Help me to recognize the
times You make a way for me—even the smallest
of blessings. Help me to know Your Word and
follow all Your instructions. You favor me and
also give me favor with others. Forgive me when
I've chosen my own way or responded selfishly.
I don't want a life of compromise; instead,
I want Your very best. I choose to put You first.
As I do so, I thank You for making a way
for me to experience great success—not
so I can say, "Look at me," but to bring
You pleasure in the way I live my life.

PROMISE KEEPER

,,

His disciples said, "Ah, now You are speaking plainly to us and not in figures of speech! Now we know that You know all things, and have no need for anyone to question You; because of this we believe [without any doubt] that you came from God." Jesus answered them, "Do you now [at last] believe? Take careful notice: an hour is coming, and has arrived, when you will all be scattered, each to his own home, leaving Me alone; and yet I am not alone, because the Father is with Me. I have told you these things, so that in Me you may have [perfect] peace. In the world you have tribulation and distress and suffering, but be courageous [be confident, be undaunted, be filled with joy]; I have overcome the world." [My conquest is accomplished, My victory abiding.]

JOHN 16:29–33 AMP

,,

- Jesus warned His disciples in His last moments on earth about persecution that would come and promised they would not be alone. How does it make you feel knowing that no matter what adversity you experience in this life, you never face it alone?
- The Holy Spirit is your Comforter, Helper, and Teacher. When has the Spirit been with you in good times and bad?
- Jesus instructed His disciples to take courage. What struggles are you facing? How do you "take courage" in the face of all that opposes you?
- There are times we all feel alone. What evidence in your life demonstrates Jesus' faithful promise to be with you always?
- When you are down, what does it mean to you to know that Jesus overcame the world?
- Through Jesus' victory, you are also an overcomer. How does that revelation encourage you in your faith and in your present situation today?

Jesus, You are with me always, even when I feel alone. My feelings can deceive me, so I must trust You and be encouraged because You are a faithful promise keeper. You know my struggles. You understand me even better than I understand myself. I live in a fallen world. There will always be difficult times in this world. I remember the times You have saved me, pulled me out of the mess I was in, and brought victory in a situation that otherwise was hopeless. No matter what opposition I face, what adversity stands against me, You are my hope and my salvation. The battle is already won. I receive Your peace and hold fast to Your promise that I am made an overcomer through Your victory!

WHEN YOU DON'T KNOW
WHAT TO PRAY

And so this is still a live promise. It wasn't canceled at the time of Joshua; otherwise, God wouldn't keep renewing the appointment for "today." The promise of "arrival" and "rest" is still there for God's people. God himself is at rest. And at the end of the journey we'll surely rest with God. So let's keep at it and eventually arrive at the place of rest, not drop out through some sort of disobedience. God means what he says. What he says goes. His powerful Word is sharp as a surgeon's scalpel, cutting through everything, whether doubt or defense, laying us open to listen and obey. Nothing and no one is impervious to God's Word. We can't get away from it—no matter what.

HEBREWS 4:8–13 MSG

- Life often presents those moments when there are no words. When have you felt like you had no words to say in prayer?
- What did you do? Did you search God's scripture for words?
- Have you considered praying God's own words back to Him?
- The Bible is filled with promises spoken from God. When have you made God's promises personal for your life?
- How do you feel when you speak the Word of God in prayer?
- How does hearing the Word of God spoken aloud concerning your situation make you feel? How does it change your perspective about whatever circumstances you are facing?
- When have the words of God seemed to come alive within you?
- What particular promises speak to your heart most frequently?
- How do you express those promises on a daily basis to God? To others? To yourself?

God, Your word moves mountains and causes oceans to stand still. When my world seems to shake within me, remind me that You have the whole world in Your hands. I don't have to do anything on my own. My circumstances turn out for my good in the end when I ask for Your help. So today I ask boldly, believing without a second thought that You hear my prayer and answer my call. Even when I feel like the answers are not coming, I will stand strong in faith and believe You have already put things into motion and are at work on my behalf. You know me and You make perfect the things that concern me. My heart is at rest knowing that You love and care for me. Your favor goes before me. I will not be consumed by the ways of the world but lift my eyes to watch You perform wonders in my life. Thank You!

SHUT THE DOOR

Humble yourselves, therefore, under God's mighty hand, that he may lift you up in due time. Cast all your anxiety on him because he cares for you. Be alert and of sober mind. Your enemy the devil prowls around like a roaring lion looking for someone to devour. Resist him, standing firm in the faith, because you know that the family of believers throughout the world is undergoing the same kind of sufferings. And the God of all grace, who called you to his eternal glory in Christ, after you have suffered a little while, will himself restore you and make you strong, firm and steadfast.

1 Peter 5:6–10 NIV

- You live in a fallen world and have an enemy seeking to destroy you, but your heavenly Father wants you to be wise and live within His protection. When have you experienced God's protection?

- You would never knowingly give the devil an open door to your life, and yet there are times he finds a way in. What things open the door to the enemy?

- Have you been so angry you couldn't see straight? When has your anger given the devil an opportunity to do you harm?

- What about disobedience? Have you knowingly done what you wanted to instead of following God's commands? When? How did that turn out?

- What about unforgiveness? Are you holding a grudge against someone? What do you think that is doing to your heart? To your relationship with God?

- Sin separates us from God. What do you need to let go of today?

Lord, I know I have an enemy, and I don't want to give him any opportunity to have a part in my life. I know that bad things happen to good people, and when something bad happens to someone, I don't believe that it's a result of sin, but Your Word says for me to examine my heart. Lord, shine Your light into my very soul and bring to light any sin in my life. Forgive me for the grudges I have held against others. I choose to forgive them. My forgiveness is not an admission that what they did was right but a demonstration that I am letting go of it so I can be free. I let go of any anger I've held on to. I will not give the devil an open door in my life. I pray a hedge of protection around me and those I love. I thank You for Your angels that stand guard, keeping me in all my ways.

PRAY—EVEN FOR THE LITTLE THINGS

"I am the true Vine, and my Father is the Gardener. He lops off every branch that doesn't produce. And he prunes those branches that bear fruit for even larger crops. He has already tended you by pruning you back for greater strength and usefulness by means of the commands I gave you. Take care to live in me, and let me live in you. For a branch can't produce fruit when severed from the vine. Nor can you be fruitful apart from me. Yes, I am the Vine; you are the branches. Whoever lives in me and I in him shall produce a large crop of fruit. For apart from me you can't do a thing. If anyone separates from me, he is thrown away like a useless branch, withers, and is gathered into a pile with all the others and burned. But if you stay in me and obey my commands, you may ask any request you like, and it will be granted!"

JOHN 15:1–7 TLB

- Do you talk to God about everything?
- If not, what kind of things do you hold back from Him? Why?
- Do you think God is too busy to be bothered with some things—things that you should be able to do on your own, like looking for something you've lost?
- What do you think Jesus meant when He said to live in Him?
- What does that look like in your life?
- How do you see Jesus living in you and through you?
- Did Jesus really mean you can ask Him anything and it will be granted?
- Is that hard to accept?
- What causes you to stumble over this truth?
- How can you change your mind-set if this is a struggle for you?
- What is something you've been trying to work out on your own that you now realize you can ask of God?

Lord, forgive me when I think I can handle things on my own. You are my everything. Without You I really can do nothing. And why would I want to do things on my own? When I live each day to please You, tapping into Your wisdom and understanding, I am more than I could ever be on my own. Teach me, Lord, to live in You. Show me how to give myself to You in a way that brings pleasure to You and good fruit into my life. I will pray about everything, giving You the opportunity to be a part of everything I do. When I am concerned about something, I will ask You about it. You have the answer I need.

THE PEACEMAKERS

·|·|·|·|·|·|·|·|·|·|·|·|·|·|·|·|·|·|·|·|·|·|·|·|·|·|·|·|·|·|·|·|·|·|·|·|·|·|·|·|·|·|·|·|·|·|·|·|·|

*"Blessed [anticipating God's presence, spiritually mature] are
the pure in heart [those with integrity, moral courage, and godly
character], for they will see God. Blessed [spiritually calm with
life-joy in God's favor] are the makers and maintainers of peace,
for they will [express His character and] be called the sons of
God. Blessed [comforted by inner peace and God's love] are those
who are persecuted for doing that which is morally right, for theirs
is the kingdom of heaven [both now and forever]. Blessed [morally
courageous and spiritually alive with life-joy in God's goodness]
are you when people insult you and persecute you, and falsely say
all kinds of evil things against you because of [your association
with] Me. Be glad and exceedingly joyful, for your reward
in heaven is great [absolutely inexhaustible]."*

MATTHEW 5:8–12 AMP

·|·|·|·|·|·|·|·|·|·|·|·|·|·|·|·|·|·|·|·|·|·|·|·|·|·|·|·|·|·|·|·|·|·|·|·|·|·|·|·|·|·|·|·|·|·|·|·|·|

- Jesus said those who choose peace are blessed and called the children of God. As a peacemaker, your joy does not depend on outward circumstances. Do you recall a time when your joy overflowed in spite of the difficulty you were experiencing?

- Do you consider yourself a peacemaker?

- As a child of God, you are called to live by a different set of principles. How are your principles different from the various cultural philosophies when it comes to peace?

- Because your motivation is different from the world's, how do you respond to betrayal?

- What inner struggle do you experience when you have to forgive someone who has hurt you or someone you love?

- In what ways do you strive for peace?

- Is your peace something others recognize in you? Why or why not?

Lord, I knew when I chose to give my life to You that things would be different, and I am so thankful for that. But our world is a difficult place to live, because living a life according to the kingdom of God means choosing to live contrary to the world's ways. It is human nature—the world's way—to live in conflict, in turmoil, stirring up strife and division. But I choose peace today. I will choose to be a peacemaker. That doesn't mean letting others walk over me and take advantage of me, but it means resolving conflicts in a way that looks different. Because I am God's child, I don't have to live the world's way. I choose today to rise above whatever issues are going on in my life and around me and celebrate the hope and joy found in You.

GOD HAS NOT FORGOTTEN YOU

,,,

*This is what the LORD says: "In the time of my favor I will answer
you, and in the day of salvation I will help you; I will keep you
and will make you to be a covenant for the people, to restore
the land and to reassign its desolate inheritances, to say to the
captives, 'Come out,' and to those in darkness, 'Be free!' They will
feed beside the roads and find pasture on every barren hill. They
will neither hunger nor thirst, nor will the desert heat or the sun
beat down on them. He who has compassion on them will guide
them." . . . But Zion said, "The LORD has forsaken me, the Lord
has forgotten me." "Can a mother forget the baby at her
breast and have no compassion on the child she has borne?
Though she may forget, I will not forget you! See,
I have engraved you on the palms of my hands."*

ISAIAH 49:8–10, 14–16 NIV

,,,

- Jesus knew He stood on the brink of the biggest battle of His earthly life as He prayed in the garden of Gethsemane. When have you felt desperately alone?
- Jesus craved companionship from His friends, but they were not there. Have you reached for the support of your friends only to find them no longer there?
- Have you ever felt like God had forgotten you?
- How do you encourage yourself in the Lord when you feel like everyone has abandoned you?
- How do you build your faith back up when those you have leaned on seem far away?
- Jesus faced death, burial, and resurrection isolated, but not alone. What can you do or say that helps you know God will never abandon you?
- What words of the Bible, or past testimonies of faith, encourage you to stand strong through even the most difficult times?

Heavenly Father, no matter what circumstances I face in this life, no matter how alone I feel, the truth is You will never leave me nor forsake me. You've promised to always be with me—always. When I don't feel Your presence or am tempted to doubt, remind me of Your Word. Whisper those precious promises into my heart. Remind me of the times when You brought light and life into my situation after what seemed like the darkest of nights. May my faith remain unshaken; may my trust in You never waver. You are the one I count on to get me through. When I raise my head in the midst of the battle, I will see You fighting for me. I am never alone.

THE LIVING, BREATHING CHURCH

,,

He said to them, "But who do you say that I am?" Simon Peter
replied, "You are the Christ. . . the Son of the living God."
Then Jesus answered him, "Blessed. . .are you, Simon son of
Jonah, because flesh and blood. . .did not reveal this to you,
but My Father who is in heaven. And I say to you that you are
Peter, and on this rock I will build My church; and the gates
of Hades (death) will not overpower it [by preventing the
resurrection of the Christ]. I will give you the keys (authority)
of the kingdom of heaven; and whatever you bind [forbid,
declare to be improper and unlawful] on earth will have
[already] been bound in heaven, and whatever you loose
[permit, declare lawful] on earth will have [already] been
loosed in heaven." Then He gave the disciples strict
orders to tell no one that He was the Christ.

MATTHEW 16:15–20 AMP

,,

- When Jesus referred to the church, He was talking about the living, breathing relationships believers have with one another. Do you have a church you belong to?

- If you don't have a church home, do you have people in your life who share your faith?

- Is your church a place where you feel comfortable doing life with those who share your faith?

- There is strength in shared faith. When was a time you felt loved, supported, or strengthened by fellow believers?

- As believers come together, they grow in every area of their lives. When was the last time you learned something new from another believer?

- If you are a part of a church, how have you grown in wisdom and understanding through the exchange of God's Word?

- Do you pray for your spiritual mentors? Do you think they need your prayers? Why or why not?

God, thank You for the church, a family of people who share my faith. I appreciate those You have placed in my life. Help me to know which relationships are divinely appointed by You. Give me wisdom to become planted firmly in a place where my faith can grow. Give me teachers and mentors that help me to become all You've created me to be. Show me how to share my faith in a way that helps others grow closer to You too. I pray for the leaders You've placed in my life. I believe they hear Your voice and follow Your instruction. Thank You for providing them with the resources they need to meet the needs of our church family in every area of life.

USE CONFLICT FOR GOOD

....

"If your brother sins against you, go and tell him his fault between you and him alone. If he hears you, you have gained your brother. But if he will not hear, take with you one or two more, that 'by the mouth of two or three witnesses every word may be established.' And if he refuses to hear them, tell it to the church. But if he refuses even to hear the church, let him be to you like a heathen and a tax collector. . . . whatever you bind on earth will be bound in heaven, and whatever you loose on earth will be loosed in heaven. . . . If two of you agree on earth concerning anything that they ask, it will be done for them by My Father in heaven."

MATTHEW 18:15–19 NKJV

....

- Do you "fight" well? Conflict doesn't have to be a negative experience.
- How do you feel when conflict arises? What emotions rise first? Why?
- When someone hurts you, is your first impulse to retaliate? What if you gave them the benefit of the doubt that something else was going on?
- What if you considered that the conflict arose from a past wound in their heart (or yours) that somehow got ripped open, and has little to nothing to do with you? Does that change your perspective?
- Jesus wants us to respond to all things with love. Why do you think that is?
- Do you find it difficult to address conflict?
- What has worked best in the past for you to resolve conflict?
- When has conflict, handled well, resulted in a stronger relationship with the other person?

Jesus, Your very mission on this earth was to provide a way for us all to be reconciled to the Father. While it's natural for us to become defensive or angry or to take it personally when conflict arises, it's not Your way. You want us to respond with love and concern for one another. Teach me by Your Holy Spirit to be one who seeks to reconcile. Help me to speak the truth in love. Open my eyes to see things from a perspective that is different from my own. When I feel hurt or wronged, I will check my emotions and take a step back. Show me how I can use conflict to benefit others and grow my relationships with them.

GOD—YOUR ROCK, YOUR STRENGTH

God's way is perfect! The promise of the LORD has proven to be true. He is a shield to all those who take refuge in him. Who is God but the LORD? Who is a rock except our God? God arms me with strength and makes my way perfect. He makes my feet like those of a deer and gives me sure footing on high places. He trains my hands for battle so that my arms can bend an archer's bow of bronze. You have given me the shield of your salvation. Your right hand supports me. Your gentleness makes me great. You make a wide path for me to walk on so that my feet do not slip.

PSALM 18:30–36 GW

- David, a mighty warrior, knew his victories were not his own. During the battle he looked to God, his rock, his safe place, his shield, and his power. Can you recall times in your life when God has been your rock?

- When was the last time you stood firmly attached to God, your rock, unmovable in your faith because you knew God was fighting for you?

- When has God provided you with a place of safety, hidden from all who oppose you? What mighty work did He do on your behalf?

- God doesn't remove the obstacles in life but instead gives you the courage to meet those challenges. What have you learned from the difficult parts of your journey?

- Would you say you have more courage? Why?

- What has God taught you through the battles?

- When you see another battle on the horizon, how do you approach it?

God, You are my rock, my salvation, and my strength. It has not been easy, and I've not always made the right choice, but You have been faithful. When I've fallen, You've always been there to pick me up. I take courage in the victories You've given me. I build on Your faithfulness, trusting that I don't have to make this journey alone. Thank You for the difficulties I've traveled, because I have learned great things along the way. I have grown in my relationship with You. You have helped me climb mountains I never thought possible. You stand with me, reassuring me and showing me the right way. I'm encouraged today knowing that the battle is not mine but Yours. You will fight for me. Your way is perfect. I will forever follow You!

FAITH STEPS

||||||||||||||||||||||||||||||||||||||||||||||||||||||||||||||||||||||||||||

*Consider it a sheer gift, friends, when tests and challenges come
at you from all sides. You know that under pressure, your faith-
life is forced into the open and shows its true colors. So don't
try to get out of anything prematurely. Let it do its work so you
become mature and well-developed, not deficient in any way.
If you don't know what you're doing, pray to the Father. He loves
to help. You'll get his help, and won't be condescended to when
you ask for it. Ask boldly, believingly, without a second thought.
People who "worry their prayers" are like wind-whipped waves.
Don't think you're going to get anything from the Master that
way, adrift at sea, keeping all your options open.*

Ʝᴀᴍᴇꜱ 1:2–8 ᴍꜱɢ

||||||||||||||||||||||||||||||||||||||||||||||||||||||||||||||||||||||||||||

- When trouble comes, what are the first thoughts that cross
  your mind?
- How do your emotions play a part in your reactions to difficult news?
- How do you battle thoughts that are contrary to God's
  Word?
- It can be hard to see a trial as a gift. When has a trial
  you've faced become a gift to you in the end? What did
  you receive from that trial?
- It's one thing to say you believe; it's another to take action
  not knowing the outcome. When have you acted in faith,
  totally relying on God to bring you through? What did you
  learn about yourself? About God?
- How does your trust in Him change as His faithfulness proves
  true after each trial?
- In what ways have you helped others stand in faith through
  a trial?

*Lord, forgive me when my thoughts falter
and I am tempted to see Your Word as mere
advice. Help me not to waver between my
feelings, the world's ideas, and Your truth.
I choose You. I am committed to You, trusting
You for Your very best in my life, realizing that
sometimes I get in my own way. I know that
my faith makes a difference. Help me to settle
my emotions and not allow them to lead me.
Open my eyes and help me to see the ways
in which I can put my faith to work. Help me
to see the evidence that my faith is producing
Your desire and purpose in my life. Give me
wisdom and insight into each situation so
that I may choose Your will every time.*

GOD'S WORD SPEAKS

,,,

*For the word of God is living and powerful, and sharper
than any two-edged sword, piercing even to the division of
soul and spirit, and of joints and marrow, and is a discerner of
the thoughts and intents of the heart. And there is no creature
hidden from His sight, but all things are naked and open to
the eyes of Him to whom we must give account. Seeing then
that we have a great High Priest who has passed through the
heavens, Jesus the Son of God, let us hold fast our confession.
For we do not have a High Priest who cannot sympathize with
our weaknesses, but was in all points tempted as we are,
yet without sin. Let us therefore come boldly to the
throne of grace, that we may obtain mercy
and find grace to help in time of need.*

HEBREWS 4:12–16 NKJV

,,,

- Who are some of the people in your life you admire and respect?
- Who has the authority to speak into your life and help you make decisions?
- Would you say the Bible is the ultimate authority for your life? Why or why not?
- Are there some things in the Bible that you don't follow, even though you know they are God's commands?
- When was the last time you read the Bible?
- Do you hear God's voice when you read it?
- What did God say the last time He spoke to you through the scriptures?

God, Your Word is true—not just the parts I like or want to see at work in my life, but every single word. It is not just a book of stories from the past but holds insight, instruction, and promises for my life. It is alive and active, and as I study it, it becomes living and active in my life. You created the world with words, and Your words, written for me, are important in my life. Give me a hunger to learn through my time of study. Help me to hear all that You have to say to me through the words I read in the Bible. I want to understand so that I know how to answer the questions I am faced with every day. Help me to grow in my personal relationship with You as I read Your truth. As I pray, I am listening for Your voice and expect You to speak to me. As I come to know Your Word, I come to know You more.

LIVE LIFE IN THE MOMENT

||||||||||||||||||||||||||||||||||||||||||||||||||||||||||||||||||||||||||||||

So what advantage has he who labors for the wind? All of his life he also eats in darkness [cheerlessly, without sweetness and light], with great frustration, sickness, and anger. Behold, here is what I have seen to be good and fitting: to eat and drink, and to find enjoyment in all the labor in which he labors under the sun during the few days of his life which God gives him—for this is his [allotted] reward. Also, every man to whom God has given riches and possessions, He has also given the power and ability to enjoy them and to receive [this as] his [allotted] portion and to rejoice in his labor. . . For he will not often consider the [troubled] days of his life, because God keeps him occupied and focused on the joy of his heart.

ECCLESIASTES 5:16–20 AMP

||||||||||||||||||||||||||||||||||||||||||||||||||||||||||||||||||||||||||||||

- Do you just get through the week so you can enjoy the weekend?
- Are you constantly pressing toward the next season in life because the one you're currently in overwhelms you?
- The difficult seasons often drive us to our knees. What have you been wrestling with in your present day-to-day?
- What things do you welcome as a distraction from your present?
- How can you embrace the moment called today and truly give it your full attention?
- What does God want you to see? To learn?
- You can find contentment in the moment because of your relationship with Him. Do you believe He is all you need?
- God wants you to experience the season you are in because it is His gift to you. Even if the moment isn't what you hoped, can you find joy in Him?

Heavenly Father, You know my heart.
You know my struggle to stay in the moment.
It's so much easier to think about the good
times I've experienced or to look forward
to those things I hope will be positive in the
future. Now is hard. I don't like this hard place.
But You have called me to live in the moment.
I will give thoughtful consideration to today.
What do You want me to learn? What do I
need to know? Open my heart, my eyes, and
my ears. Help me to see the things I've shut
my eyes to, and settle my soul that I might
hear the things I need to hear. This experience
means something, and I don't want to miss
the opportunity to understand. Give me
peace and strength to journey through
this season with Your perspective.

YOU MAKE ME NEW

,,,

This is what the LORD says—he who made a way through the sea, a path through the mighty waters, who drew out the chariots and horses, the army and reinforcements together, and they lay there, never to rise again, extinguished, snuffed out like a wick: "Forget the former things; do not dwell on the past. See, I am doing a new thing! Now it springs up; do you not perceive it? I am making a way in the wilderness and streams in the wasteland. The wild animals honor me, the jackals and the owls, because I provide water in the wilderness and streams in the wasteland, to give drink to my people, my chosen, the people I formed for myself that they may proclaim my praise."

ISAIAH 43:16–21 NIV

,,,

- Do you ever feel like your past defines you?
- Are you challenged to see change in your life?
- Have you ever felt like you were stuck in a place and you might never get out?
- Do you struggle to see yourself as more than the person you were before Christ?
- What do you need to do to get a better image of who you are in Christ?
- How do you think God sees you today?
- How are you different from the way you were before?
- Is there anything from your old life that you need to let go of so you can embrace the new?
- God is at work behind the scenes of your life to bring in the new season. What do you hope He is working on?

Lord, You make all things new. Thank You for all You've done so far in my life. I open up my heart to the new that You want to do. I let go of my past. I am a new creature in Christ. Help me to see myself as the new You've created me to be. I give You everything I've held on to up till now. I release it and let it go so that I can embrace You and the new You have for me. When I think about the old way I used to be and the old choices I used to make, whisper Your truth. Help me to look to You and hear the plans You have for me. I know that You are at work in my life. You have a plan and You have set a path before me. I choose Your way. I choose to focus forward and live according to the purpose You've given me. Make me new in You.

UNCONDITIONAL, NEVER-ENDING LOVE

,,

O Lord, you have examined my heart and know everything about me. . . . You chart the path ahead of me and tell me where to stop and rest. Every moment you know where I am. You know what I am going to say before I even say it. You both precede and follow me and place your hand of blessing on my head. This is too glorious, too wonderful to believe! I can never be lost to your Spirit! I can never get away from my God! If I go up to heaven, you are there; if I go down to the place of the dead, you are there. If I ride the morning winds to the farthest oceans, even there your hand will guide me, your strength will support me. If I try to hide in the darkness, the night becomes light around me. For even darkness cannot hide from God; to you the night shines as bright as day. Darkness and light are both alike to you.

PSALM 139:1–12 TLB

,,

- When you meet someone new, do you ever hide a little bit of yourself for fear that they might not like something about you?
- What does unconditional love look like to you?
- Have you experienced it, perhaps from your parents, grandparents, or someone else?
- How does it make you feel to know there is nothing you can do that could make God love you less?
- What does it mean to you never to be lost from God's presence?
- Are you going through a difficulty? What looks different to you in that circumstance as you consider that God desires His very best for you?
- Do you tell God you love Him? What words do you use?
- What expressions of thankfulness and gratitude can you share with God today?

God, thank You for loving me unconditionally. I can do nothing that would make You love me more or less. You know every single thing about me—every thought I have—good or bad. You know my dreams and aspirations, and You've experienced the dark and heavy moments of my life. Wherever I go, You are with me. I can't escape Your presence, even if I wanted to (and I don't). Whatever I need, You're there to take care of me. When I face a difficulty, help me to remember that no matter how big that problem seems to be, You are bigger. When I alone can't think of a way out, You've already made a way of escape. You have the answer before I ever had the question. I love You. Thank You for loving me with an everlasting, never-ending love.

A NEW START WITH A NEW HEART

||||||||||||||||||||||||||||||||||||||||||||||||||||||||||||||||||||||||||

"I will take you from the nations and gather you from every country. I will bring you back to your own land. I will sprinkle clean water on you and make you clean instead of unclean. Then I will cleanse you from all your idols. I will give you a new heart and put a new spirit in you. I will remove your stubborn hearts and give you obedient hearts. I will put my Spirit in you. I will enable you to live by my laws, and you will obey my rules. Then you will live in the land that I gave your ancestors. You will be my people, and I will be your God. I will rescue you from all your uncleanness. I will make the grain grow so that you will never again have famines."

EZEKIEL 36:24–29 GW

||||||||||||||||||||||||||||||||||||||||||||||||||||||||||||||||||||||||||

- Compared to the time you were without God, do you see a big difference in yourself now that He lives in you?
- Perhaps you've known God since you were a child. If so, what do you think your life might have been like without Him?
- Was there ever a time when your heart was hard as stone?
- How has God changed your heart?
- What does it mean to you to know that you belong to God?
- When have you felt unclean?
- After asking for forgiveness, how did your fresh start change your perspective?
- How do you see life differently compared to those you know who are without Christ?

Lord, I was lost without You. I could do nothing on my own, even when I thought I could. Thank You for giving me a new heart. Thank You for placing Your Spirit within me. You picked up the pieces of my life, once broken, and began again. You took the dirty, cold, and hard heart that I once had before You and made my heart new. You revived me with Your own Spirit and filled me with resurrection life. I am grateful to know that when I fail, I can have a fresh start in You. You are always at work within me, molding and shaping my heart to reflect Your image. Help me to be willing and obedient to the plans You have for me. Help me to trust that Your ways are higher and Your plans are better, even when I don't fully understand. Thank You for loving me and making me Your own. When people see me, let them see a heart like Yours.

CULTIVATE A HEART OF THANKSGIVING

I will praise you, LORD, with all my heart; before the "gods" I will sing your praise. I will bow down toward your holy temple and will praise your name for your unfailing love and your faithfulness, for you have so exalted your solemn decree that it surpasses your fame. When I called, you answered me; you greatly emboldened me. May all the kings of the earth praise you, LORD, when they hear what you have decreed. May they sing of the ways of the LORD, for the glory of the LORD is great. Though the LORD is exalted, he looks kindly on the lowly; though lofty, he sees them from afar. Though I walk in the midst of trouble, you preserve my life. You stretch out your hand against the anger of my foes; with your right hand you save me. The LORD will vindicate me; your love, LORD, endures forever—do not abandon the works of your hands.

PSALM 138 NIV

- Are you a glass half-full or half-empty kind of person? When things aren't going your way, do you allow them to steal your joy?
- When was the last time you took the good things for granted?
- When you find yourself in that place, what brings you back around to all the things you're thankful for?
- What gifts and talents has God given you?
- When was the last time you celebrated the good God has done in your life?
- What motivates you to nurture a heart of thanksgiving?
- What are you thankful for today? Make a list.
- How do you express your thankfulness to God?

Heavenly Father, I never want to take Your blessings for granted. Even life and breath are things I am thankful to You for. Each day is a gift. No matter what challenges I face, I never have to face them without You. Today I bring my list of blessings to You in prayer. I take time today to list each one. You have given me much, beginning with the life of Your only Son in exchange for mine. I refuse to let disappointment steal my joy. My joy is a decision just like my faith. I choose Your joy today. I am thankful I don't have to pretend that all is well. Like the psalmist David, I am free to share my challenges with You. But in the end, I will remember to count it all joy because of the great and mighty God I serve. In the end, we win!

THE HEARTBEAT OF COMPASSION

Jesus replied with an illustration: "A Jew going on a trip from Jerusalem to Jericho was attacked by bandits. They stripped him of his clothes and money, and beat him up and left him lying half dead beside the road. By chance a Jewish priest came along; and when he saw the man lying there, he crossed to the other side of the road and passed him by. A Jewish Temple-assistant walked over and looked at him lying there, but then went on. But a despised Samaritan came along, and when he saw him, he felt deep pity. Kneeling beside him the Samaritan soothed his wounds with medicine and bandaged them. Then he put the man on his donkey and walked along beside him till they came to an inn, where he nursed him through the night. The next day he handed the innkeeper two twenty-dollar bills and told him to take care of the man. 'If his bill runs higher than that,' he said, 'I'll pay the difference the next time I am here.' "

LUKE 10:30–35 TLB

- What motivates your actions each day?
- When you see someone in need, how do you generally respond?
- Would you say you are a compassionate person? Why or why not?
- If you had seen this man from Jesus' parable, what do you believe you would have done? Would you have intervened?
- Does the love of God move you to touch the untouchables, to accept the excluded, and to see those society prefers to remain invisible?
- Would God say that you have a heart that reflects His when it comes to having compassion for others?
- Do you talk to God about what He would like you to do in these situations?

Jesus, thank You for Your compassion for all of us, especially for showing compassion to me. I could have been unlovable to some, but not to You. Forgive me for closing my eyes to the pain others experience, for looking away or pretending they are invisible. I want to see them, and I want them to know by my actions that You see them. Let Your Spirit living inside me open my eyes to see how I can show others Your love. Help me to step outside myself and express Your compassion to others. Sometimes my own family is hard to show love to. I want to be Your hands and feet to those You bring across my path. Give me wisdom to hear those You'd have me help and to say the words to them You'd have me say. Help me to respond with a heart like Yours.

YOU SHALL NOT BE OVERCOME

,,,

And do not become idolaters as were some of them. As it is written, "The people sat down to eat and drink, and rose up to play." Nor let us commit sexual immorality, as some of them did, and in one day twenty-three thousand fell; nor let us tempt Christ, as some of them also tempted, and were destroyed by serpents; nor complain, as some of them also complained, and were destroyed by the destroyer. Now all these things happened to them as examples, and they were written for our admonition, upon whom the ends of the ages have come. Therefore let him who thinks he stands take heed lest he fall. No temptation has overtaken you except such as is common to man; but God is faithful, who will not allow you to be tempted beyond what you are able, but with the temptation will also make the way of escape, that you may be able to bear it.

1 CORINTHIANS 10:7–13 NKJV

,,,

- Throughout history God continues to rescue His people, not because we deserve it but because He loves us. When has God rescued you?
- When the pressure of temptation feels like it's too much, do you ever feel singled out?
- How can you remind yourself that we all face wrong desires and that you've not been singled out?
- When has God given you insight to recognize people and situations that you should avoid?
- How have you handled those who have a negative, ungodly influence in your life?
- When have you run from something you knew was wrong?
- Have you ever felt trapped, but then God provided a way out? How did that influence your relationship with God?

Jesus, You sent the Holy Spirit to be with me, to lead and guide me. I open my heart to hear the wisdom of the Holy Spirit concerning those things that are wrong for me. Forgive me today for those things I've given in to in the past. Thank You for helping me to overcome those things. Thank You for freeing me from any bondage to the sins of my past. In the midst of any situation, I know You have provided me with a way out. Make that path clear to me. Thank You for friends who love me and love You. I seek refuge in their encouragement and godly counsel. I put my heart on notice today to be alert. I will recognize a tempting situation and remove myself from it immediately.

JESUS' PRAYER FOR YOU

‚‚

"I'm also praying for those who will believe in me through their
message. I pray that all of these people continue to have unity
in the way that you, Father, are in me and I am in you. I pray
that they may be united with us so that the world will believe
that you have sent me. I have given them the glory that you
gave me. I did this so that they are united in the same way we
are. I am in them, and you are in me. So they are completely
united. In this way the world knows that you have sent me
and that you have loved them in the same way you have
loved me. . . . I have made your name known to them,
and I will make it known so that the love you have
for me will be in them and I will be in them."

JOHN 17:20–23, 26 GW

‚‚

- Jesus prayed for you before you ever received Him. What emotions does that evoke?
- What thoughts come to mind about Jesus' thoughts toward you?
- Jesus prayed for unity so that those who follow Him would be a powerful witness in the world. Are you a witness to Him? How?
- What does it mean to you to be united with Jesus? With other believers?
- Are you working toward uniting believers in faith?
- What more could you do to demonstrate the reality of God's love to other believers and to those who don't yet know Him?
- What does Jesus' prayer for you do for your faith? Does it build your faith? Add strength to your witness?

Jesus, it encourages me to read Your prayer for me and for my brothers and sisters in faith. Thank You for believing in me and giving me the opportunity to know You. Help me to be one who unites others in faith. I want to demonstrate Your love to everyone I meet. Give me the strength and wisdom to live my life in a way that my character and faith point others to You. Purify my heart and mind each day as I read Your Word and pray. Let Your truth point out any sin, and motivate me to confess those sins to You. As I do, my relationship with You grows deeper and I can be assured that I am on the right path—Your path for me. Even when it's uncomfortable to stand for what is right and true, I desire to do it. I will stand out of the crowd and stand up for You.

FOREVER FRIENDSHIPS

IIIIIIIIIIIIIIIIIIIIIIIIIIIIIIIIIIIIIIIIIIIIIIIIIIIIIIIIIIIIIIIIIIIIIIIIIII

This is what I have asked of God for you: that you will be encouraged and knit together by strong ties of love, and that you will have the rich experience of knowing Christ with real certainty and clear understanding. . . . For though I am far away from you my heart is with you, happy because you are getting along so well, happy because of your strong faith in Christ. And now just as you trusted Christ to save you, trust him, too, for each day's problems; live in vital union with him. . . . See that you go on growing in the Lord, and become strong and vigorous in the truth you were taught. Let your lives overflow with joy and thanksgiving for all he has done.

COLOSSIANS 2:2, 5-7 TLB

IIIIIIIIIIIIIIIIIIIIIIIIIIIIIIIIIIIIIIIIIIIIIIIIIIIIIIIIIIIIIIIIIIIIIIIIIII

- Have you ever met someone and it felt like you had known them all your life even though you just met?
- Do you have relationships with friends and family that you know run deep?
- Are there relationships in your life that need to be restored? Have you lost hope in that ever happening? Ask God if any of those past relationships need to be restored. Then if you feel Him leading you, ask Him to give you opportunities to reconnect.
- It's a true gift from God when you find those people with the amazing ability to stir the gifts of God within you. Who are those people in your life?
- Are you that friend who reaches deep into the heart of another and draws out the gift inside of them?
- When was the last time you shared with that person how much they mean to you?
- If you don't have those kinds of relationships, have you asked God to give you friends like that?

Father, thank You for those divine connections, those people whose faces are before me now that I know You've put them in my life. I need people in my life who stir up the gifts You've placed in me. Give me more of those types of relationships. And thank You for allowing me to be that kind of friend to others. For those relationships that I wish were much more than they are, please reveal to me if it's Your desire for those relationship bridges to be rebuilt. Then open the door in such a way that I know it's Your plan to pursue a renewed relationship with those people.

HEART CONNECTIONS

IIIIIIIIIIIIIIIIIIIIIIIIIIIIIIIIIIIIIIIIIIIIIIIIIIIIIIIIIIIIIIIIIIIIIIIIII

Two are better than one, because they have a good return for their labor: If either of them falls down, one can help the other up. But pity anyone who falls and has no one to help them up. Also, if two lie down together, they will keep warm. But how can one keep warm alone? Though one may be overpowered, two can defend themselves. A cord of three strands is not quickly broken. . . . The purposes of a person's heart are deep waters, but one who has insight draws them out.

Ecclesiastes 4:9–12; Proverbs 20:5 niv

IIIIIIIIIIIIIIIIIIIIIIIIIIIIIIIIIIIIIIIIIIIIIIIIIIIIIIIIIIIIIIIIIIIIIIIIII

- Charles Finney said, "Nothing tends more to cement the hearts of Christians than praying together. Never do they love one another so well as when they witness the outpouring of each other's hearts in prayer." Who has God brought into your life that you share a divine connection with?
- Did you feel like you'd known them all your life?
- Was it easy to open up and share your heart with them? Why or why not?
- God gives us those relationships to reach into our hearts with conversation and questions that stir the Spirit of God within us. When was the last time you experienced that?
- If you don't have a friendship in your life like that, do you want one? Have you asked God to give you someone of His choosing?
- Are you the one God uses to reach deep into the soul of another and bring the gift inside of them into view?

Lord, thank You for the divine friendships in my life. Sometimes I get so busy, I forget to make those relationships a priority. I know that friendship is important to You, so I will give it priority. Your Word says that iron sharpens iron. I want to be sharpened by those You bring into my life. Please bring their faces before me. Impress upon my heart the right time to connect with them. Give me strength to be open and willing to hear the things You want to say to me through them. Help me to speak Your truth in love and offer encouragement just when they need it as well. Lord, I am open to receive that friend that perhaps I've overlooked or not been open to connect with. I ask that You present that opportunity to me again and prick my heart to be quick to connect. I will honor the friends You've placed in my life. I will love them and give them place to speak Your truth, for a season or always—however You lead.

HEALING AND RESTORATION

▪▪

" 'But all who devour you will be devoured; all your enemies
will go into exile. Those who plunder you will be plundered; all
who make spoil of you I will despoil. But I will restore you to
health and heal your wounds,' declares the LORD, 'because you
are called an outcast, Zion for whom no one cares.' " . . .
Praise the LORD, my soul; all my inmost being, praise his holy
name. Praise the LORD, my soul, and forget not all his benefits—
who forgives all your sins and heals all your diseases,
who redeems your life from the pit and crowns you with
love and compassion, who satisfies your desires with good
things so that your youth is renewed like the eagle's.

JEREMIAH 30:16–17; PSALM 103:1–5 NIV

▪▪

- How do your daily choices play a role in your overall health?
- Healing is important in every area of your life—spiritual, mental, physical, and emotional. Do you believe a deficiency in one area of your life impacts your health in the other areas? Why or why not?
- Jesus is most concerned about your spiritual health. Is your spiritual health your first priority?
- What distractions keep you from nurturing your spiritual health?
- When you are balanced in all areas of life, how do you feel?
- Where does it affect you most when you're unhealthy in one area?
- As for your physical health, in what areas do you struggle?
- What things are you doing to improve your physical health?

Jesus, You were beaten and bruised so that I could be healthy and whole. You took my sicknesses and weaknesses to the cross so that I could live in health. Thank You for doing that. I want to live my very best life healthy and whole in every area of my life. Forgive me, Lord, for the times I've not made wise decisions concerning my health. I want to stand firm in my decisions, and sometimes it's hard when tempted. I am committed from this day forward to do my part physically to be complete and whole. Give me the strength and determination to grow in my spiritual health, too, so that health in all the other areas of my life follows. Your Word promises healing and restoration. For all the areas of my life that are lacking, I ask You today for restoration and complete healing. I thank You for wisdom to do what is necessary to live in health all the days of my life.

FINANCIAL GOALS

Ambition and death are alike in this: neither is ever satisfied. The purity of silver and gold can be tested in a crucible, but a man is tested by his reaction to men's praise. You can't separate a rebel from his foolishness though you crush him to powder. Riches can disappear fast. And the king's crown doesn't stay in his family forever—so watch your business interests closely. Know the state of your flocks and your herds; then there will be lambs' wool enough for clothing and goats' milk enough for food for all your household after the hay is harvested, and the new crop appears, and the mountain grasses are gathered in. . . . Steady plodding brings prosperity; hasty speculation brings poverty.

PROVERBS 27:20–27; 21:5 TLB

- The Bible contains powerful strategies for handling money. Do you believe you make wise choices for your finances?
- Would you say you spend wisely and save for the future? Why or why not?
- What would you say is your biggest disappointment financially?
- What do you do well with your finances?
- What do you want to do differently?
- Do you have a budget? Do you agree that a budget is important to your future financial success?
- If you struggle with money decisions, are you open to growing in this area? Besides God's Word, where can you go for help?
- What goals have you set for your financial future?
- What are you doing each day to achieve those goals?
- What do you need from God to help you choose financial success?
- Have you taken time recently to ask God's advice?

Heavenly Father, Your Word says You have made all wisdom available to me. I want to tap into financial wisdom. I will diligently search Your Word for those precious nuggets of truth about how to make the best decisions financially. I ask You to speak to my heart and give me specific goals for my finances. Your ways are higher than my ways, and I am determined to hear Your voice and follow Your direction. I ask You today to help me plan a budget and stay committed to it. I've made wrong choices in my finances in the past. Help me to recover from those mistakes.

When I'm tempted, remind me of my commitment to You and to my goals for the future. In my buying choices, I will purchase what I need instead of what I want. I will consider first and not buy things on impulse. I will keep my eyes on the prize of financial freedom as I look to You in all I do.

PREPARED TO DO GOOD

'''

*But you must keep on believing the things you have been
taught. You know they are true, for you know that you can trust
those of us who have taught you. You know how, when you
were a small child, you were taught the holy Scriptures;
and it is these that make you wise to accept God's salvation
by trusting in Christ Jesus. The whole Bible was given to us
by inspiration from God and is useful to teach us what is true
and to make us realize what is wrong in our lives; it straightens
us out and helps us do what is right. It is God's way
of making us well prepared at every point,
fully equipped to do good to everyone.*

2 TIMOTHY 3:14–17 TLB

'''

- Do you take time to read the Bible? If so, how much time each week do you spend reading it?
- Is reading the Bible important to you? Why?
- How does God's Word inspire you?
- The Bible is a picture of all that is right and true. How does God's Word help you discern what is good and right for your life?
- How does the Bible build your confidence in God and build your faith? What examples in your life can you think of to support your answer?
- In what ways has your understanding of the Bible prepared you to live for God?
- How often do God's words come to mind as you are making decisions? How does that help you?
- How different might your life be if the Bible weren't easily accessible?

God, thank You for the Bible. I am grateful to live in a time when Your Word is so accessible. Forgive me when I've not made it a priority in my life. Help me to understand that the more I know the Word, the more I know You. Help me not only to read but to retain Your truth. May it penetrate my heart and become a part of who I am. The more truth from Your Word I retain, the better prepared I am to live my life well. I am able to help others with the understanding I have from Your Word. May Your words lead me and guide me. Please bring Your words to my heart and mind as I make this journey of faith. Inspire me with truth and wisdom as I look to You and Your Word for answers for my life.

GRACE TO THE HUMBLE

,,

*Likewise, you younger men [of lesser rank and experience],
be subject to your elders [seek their counsel]; and all of you,
clothe yourselves with humility toward one another [tie on
the servant's apron], for GOD IS OPPOSED TO THE PROUD [the
disdainful, the presumptuous, and He defeats them], BUT HE
GIVES GRACE TO THE HUMBLE. Therefore humble yourselves
under the mighty hand of God [set aside self-righteous pride],
so that He may exalt you [to a place of honor in His service] at
the appropriate time, casting all your cares [all your anxieties,
all your worries, and all your concerns, once and for
all] on Him, for He cares about you.*

1 PETER 5:5–7 AMP

,,

- Most people want a little recognition for their accomplishments and good deeds. Have you ever felt frustrated because you didn't get credit for something you worked hard for? Did it bother you when others didn't notice?

- Do you find humility a bit easier when you consider that every ability you have comes from God?

- It takes humility to give God the glory instead of taking credit on your own. Is it easy for you to truly give the credit to God for your achievements?

- God, more than anyone else in your life, knows what it takes for you to achieve something. What does it mean to you to know that God's acknowledgment counts so much more than any praise received from others?

- When have you achieved something with God's help—something you know you would never have achieved on your own?

- How does it feel to know that your success is important to God?

God, all that I am and every ability that I have comes from You. No matter what I am on my own, I am so much more because of my relationship with You. I am grateful for the gifts and talents that You've given me. When others praise me, help me to remember that it is Your supernatural power on my abilities that allows me to do these things. Thank You for taking me far beyond my limits by empowering me to do more. When I am tempted to say, "Look at me; look what I've done," remind me that You give grace to the humble. Instead of pointing to myself, I want to point to You. Help me to look to You when I am frustrated with others. In due season, You will lift me up and give me success. Thank You for those You've placed in my life—and in my profession—who encourage me. Each success I have is Your success.

GOD WANTS TO USE YOU

*Then Jonah prayed to the LORD his God from the fish's belly. And
he said: "I cried out to the LORD because of my affliction, and He
answered me. . . . The waters surrounded me, even to my soul; the
deep closed around me; weeds were wrapped around my head.
I went down to the moorings of the mountains; the earth with its
bars closed behind me forever; yet You have brought up my life
from the pit, O LORD, my God. When my soul fainted within me,
I remembered the LORD; and my prayer went up to You, into Your
holy temple. Those who regard worthless idols forsake their own
Mercy. But I will sacrifice to You with the voice of thanksgiving;
I will pay what I have vowed. Salvation is of the LORD."*

JONAH 2:1-2, 5-9 NKJV

- When Jonah found himself near death in the belly of a whale, he remembered God and cried for help. Would you say that when times are going well, you find yourself spending less time on your knees?

- God wanted to use Jonah to save people Jonah despised. Have you ever felt like God wanted to use you to help someone you didn't particularly like?

- Can you remember a time when you took God for granted? Why did you?

- What caused you to reach out to Him?

- Jonah's prayer is filled with thanksgiving. Aside from your salvation, when has God saved you?

- God used a variety of life's circumstances to bring Jonah's will into agreement with His plan, from a violent storm to a whale that swallowed Jonah. What adversity have you faced that brought you to a better understanding of God's plan for your life?

- How does God want to use you today?

God, You are faithful and true. No matter where in the world I am, no matter what circumstance I face, You hear me. Even from the belly of a whale, You listen to my prayer. I am so thankful for the path You've placed me on. I will look to You in the good and bad times. I will speak to You as I do my close friends and include You in my everyday life. I celebrate You in both the blessings and the adversity. I am thankful for my firm foundation. I walk by faith, following You at every turn. When You speak, I will listen. When You tell me to go, I will go. When You tell me to wait, I will wait, no matter how much it tries my patience. Use me today to lead others into a relationship with You.

WHEN THE HEART NEEDS ENCOURAGEMENT

Now the company of believers was of one heart and soul, and not one [of them] claimed that anything belonging to him was [exclusively] his own, but everything was common property and for the use of all. And with great ability and power the apostles were continuously testifying to the resurrection of the Lord Jesus, and great grace rested richly upon them all. There was not a needy person among them, because those who were owners of land or houses were selling them, and bringing the proceeds of the sales and placing the money down at the apostles' feet. Then it was distributed to each as anyone had need. Now Joseph. . .who was surnamed Barnabas by the apostles (which translated means Son of Encouragement), sold a field belonging to him and brought the money and set it at the apostles' feet.

Acts 4:32-37 AMP

- Without encouragement in the middle of adversity, hope dissipates. When have you felt like giving up and an unexpected spark of encouragement gave you inspiration to continue?
- How did that breath of hope help you make it through?
- In what amazing ways have you received encouragement?
- Who are the specific people God has used to give you the hope you needed just in time?
- Does it help you to remember that your struggle is not against flesh and blood but against the spiritual forces of evil in the heavenly realms (Ephesians 6:12)? How does it change your perspective on what you're going through? Why?
- In what ways do you respond to those who encourage you?
- Is there someone in your life today who needs encouragement? Pray for them and ask God what you can do for them.

*Lord, thank You for sending encouragement
at just the right time. Whether it's a scripture
You bring to my mind, a memory of Your
faithfulness, or a person who speaks Your
good into my heart and mind, thank You! I
am often tempted to react to the pressure of
feeling hopeless with an emotional outburst.
And sometimes I do. I am grateful that I can
be honest and share how I feel with You.
When I think about the spiritual battle going
on in this world, it helps me to realize that
there is more to this situation than I can see.
I know that You are on my side through all of
this. Help me to be an encourager to others.
I want to be more aware of when others
need encouragement. Use me in a
way that brings hope to their lives.*

ABOVE ALL, PLEASE CHRIST

Figure out what will please Christ, and then do it. Don't waste your time on useless work, mere busywork, the barren pursuits of darkness. Expose these things for the sham they are. It's a scandal when people waste their lives on things they must do in the darkness where no one will see. Rip the cover off those frauds and see how attractive they look in the light of Christ. Wake up from your sleep, climb out of your coffins; Christ will show you the light! So watch your step. Use your head. Make the most of every chance you get. These are desperate times! Don't live carelessly, unthinkingly. Make sure you understand what the Master wants.

Ephesians 5:10-17 msg

- What's your purpose? Why are you here on this earth? It's a question people spend their whole lives asking. Do you know?
- What are you most passionate about? Is that your purpose?
- Sometimes we can make the answer to that question more complex than it needs to be. Is that the case for you?
- The apostle Paul accomplished an astounding amount in two decades of ministry. What made him tick? What drove him to carry out the work that he did? (See Philippians 3:7–9.)
- Paul lived to know Christ by following Him in all things, and then he encouraged others to follow him as he followed Christ. He simply set the best example he could. What examples are you setting for those watching your life?
- Have you made mistakes? Paul did too.
- When he fell, Paul picked himself up, took ownership of his mistakes, and pressed on. Is that difficult for you?
- What changes do you need to make to pursue Christ above all else?

Jesus, above all else, I do want to follow You.
I know I've put my focus on so many other
things, but truly You are the most important
relationship I have. I realize today that when
I live to please You instead of myself or
others, everything falls into place. It's not
always easy, but it's right. Following You puts
me in the right place at the right time for Your
purpose for my life to be complete. I will strive
to be that person that lives as the example
for others. I recognize I will make mistakes.
I will fail at times. Help me to get back up
and take ownership of my mistakes. I want to
be responsible to You and to others. Give me
grace to live humbly before You and
those who are watching my life.
Above all else, I want to please You.

AN OVERFLOWING HEART

*"A good man brings good things out of the good stored up
in his heart, and an evil man brings evil things out of the evil
stored up in his heart. For the mouth speaks what the heart is
full of. Why do you call me, 'Lord, Lord,' and do not do what
I say? As for everyone who comes to me and hears my words
and puts them into practice, I will show you what they are like.
They are like a man building a house, who dug down deep and
laid the foundation on rock. When a flood came, the torrent
struck that house but could not shake it, because it was well
built. But the one who hears my words and does not put them
into practice is like a man who built a house on the ground
without a foundation. The moment the torrent struck that
house, it collapsed and its destruction was complete."*

LUKE 6:45–49 NIV

- Can you think of a few reasons why someone would build a house without establishing a firm foundation?
- Sometimes people take the road that seems easiest but leaves the foundation of their heart without substance. Are you ever tempted to take the easy way and follow the crowd?
- When life is calm, the foundation of your life doesn't seem to matter; but when the storms rise, it's then that your foundation matters. Have you faced storms?
- How have storms caused you to dig deep?
- Have storms in the past revealed a need for a stronger foundation?
- Jesus said whatever you've stored up in your heart eventually comes out. Have you experienced that in your own life? In the lives of friends or coworkers?
- What do you want to have overflow from your heart? How are you filling up with that?

Jesus, You know my heart. You can see every area of my life and how I am building it. I ask You today to reach deep into the places of my heart that perhaps I want to forget or tried to hide from You—and even from myself. Shine the light of Your love on things I need to work on, places that need work. I know it might not be easy to look at those things, but it is time for me to address them. Point out the changes I need to make to be successful in my relationship with You and with others, and give me the strength to make those changes. Show me how to fill my life with the good things that You want to overflow into the lives of others.

THANKFUL IN ALL THINGS

,,,

I see God moving across the deserts from Mount Sinai.
His brilliant splendor fills the earth and sky; his glory fills the
heavens, and the earth is full of his praise! What a wonderful
God he is! From his hands flash rays of brilliant light. He
rejoices in his awesome power. Pestilence marches before
him; plague follows close behind. He stops; he stands still for
a moment, gazing at the earth. Then he shakes the nations,
scattering the everlasting mountains and leveling the hills.
His power is just the same as always! . . . Even though the fig
trees are all destroyed, and there is neither blossom left nor
fruit; though the olive crops all fail, and the fields lie barren;
even if the flocks die in the fields and the cattle barns are
empty, yet I will rejoice in the Lord; I will be happy in the God
of my salvation. The Lord God is my strength; he will give me
the speed of a deer and bring me safely over the mountains.

HABAKKUK 3:3-6, 17-19 TLB

,,,

- Do you feel like the events happening around you control your feelings, your mood, or your attitude?
- The world is fallen, dark, and sometimes heartbreaking. When bad things happen, especially to good people, do you find it difficult to trust God?
- Do hard times challenge your faith or cause you to lose your joy?
- Habakkuk had questions like ours today—why do those who choose to do evil seem to thrive while those who do good suffer? God answered: they don't, at least not in the long run. What gives you confidence and hope in this confusing world?
- Even in the worst of times, are you able to thank God for answering your prayers, for His provision to meet your needs, or for His ability to keep you safe and protected?

God, I can easily let the events happening around me get the best of me. Forgive me when I assume things I should not. Remind me that I can come to You with questions about the things going on in my life and going on around me. I open my heart and my mind to hear the answers. Help me to settle my heart and become peaceful in the middle of the chaos. You are my peace. I can remain joyful because joy, like faith, doesn't depend on my circumstances. I am thankful for my relationship with You. I am thankful for who You are and who You've created me to be. Although the journey isn't easy, I am grateful that You're using it so that I will become all You desire me to be. Thank You!

LET YOUR LOVE RUN DEEP

Let love of your fellow believers continue. Do not neglect to extend hospitality to strangers [especially among the family of believers—being friendly, cordial, and gracious, sharing the comforts of your home and doing your part generously], for by this some have entertained angels without knowing it. Remember those who are in prison, as if you were their fellow prisoner, and those who are mistreated, since you also are in the body [and subject to physical suffering].... Let your character [your moral essence, your inner nature] be free from the love of money [shun greed—be financially ethical], being content with what you have; for He has said, "I WILL NEVER [under any circumstances] DESERT YOU [nor give you up nor leave you without support, nor will I in any degree leave you helpless], NOR WILL I FORSAKE OR LET YOU DOWN OR RELAX MY HOLD ON YOU [assuredly not]!"

HEBREWS 13:1–3, 5 AMP

- Would you say you grew up in a family that showed affection or said, "I love you," to one another?

- How does that impact your ability to demonstrate love to others—those you know, as well as strangers?

- Genuine love for others produces tangible actions. Does your love demonstrate friendliness, warmth, kindness? What about understanding and compassion?

- Do you offer your kindness freely to those you don't know, even those society pretends are invisible?

- How might you communicate to those the world looks away from that you see them?

- Do others consider you loyal, reliable, and trustworthy?

- Are you approachable?

- Recall times when you showed God's love to a stranger. How did you feel?

Jesus, while on this earth You demonstrated
the Father's love for all of us. Your actions
demonstrated that love as You reached out
and touched the lives of all who would draw
near to You. Often You went to them so they
could see their value to You and to the Father.
I want to offer others a love that runs deep
from the Father's heart through mine. Teach
me how to be more compassionate and kind.
Help me to reach out in simple ways to give
kindness and grace to everyone. I don't want
to be selfish and self-absorbed. Help me
know how to show those who sometimes feel
invisible to the world that I see them. . .
and You see them too. Open my eyes
to a higher perspective. Give me a
glimpse of how You see my world.

SPIRIT OF THE LIVING GOD

....

*For those who live according to the flesh set their minds on
the things of the flesh, but those who live according to the
Spirit, the things of the Spirit. For to be carnally minded is
death, but to be spiritually minded is life and peace. Because
the carnal mind is enmity against God; for it is not subject to
the law of God, nor indeed can be. So then, those who are in
the flesh cannot please God. But you are not in the flesh but
in the Spirit, if indeed the Spirit of God dwells in you. Now if
anyone does not have the Spirit of Christ, he is not His. And if
Christ is in you, the body is dead because of sin, but the Spirit
is life because of righteousness. But if the Spirit of Him who
raised Jesus from the dead dwells in you, He who raised
Christ from the dead will also give life to your mortal
bodies through His Spirit who dwells in you.*

ROMANS 8:5–11 NKJV

....

- If you have trusted Christ for your salvation and invited Him
  to live in you, there is no doubt you are saved. Have you
  received Him fully and acknowledged Him as your Lord? If
  so, the same Spirit that raised Christ from the dead lives in
  you. What does that mean to you personally?
- Have you noticed a deeper desire to know God?
- How have you made different choices because of your
  decision to accept Christ?
- What changes have taken place in the way you pray or in
  your desire to pray?
- In what ways do you see the power of the Holy Spirit at work
  in your life? (If you don't see evidence of His work, ask God
  to begin to show you today.)

*Jesus, thank You for sending the Holy Spirit
to me. I have assurance of my salvation.
I refuse to believe the lies when the enemy
tries to bring doubt and confusion. I trust
You, knowing that I will spend eternity with
You. Eternity begins now. The Holy Spirit is
at work leading, guiding, and directing my
life. Open my eyes and help me to see where
He is at work. Show me even the smallest
of things that You are doing to bring about
Your purpose and plan for my life. You are my
Lord, and I give each day to You. I will live
according to Your Word and do what You've
asked me to do. I have joy each day because
of the changes You have made in my life.
I welcome the Holy Spirit to continue
to mold and shape me in Your image.*

GIVING SINCERELY

Because of the kindness that God has shown me, I ask you not to think of yourselves more highly than you should. Instead, your thoughts should lead you to use good judgment based on what God has given each of you as believers. Our bodies have many parts, but these parts don't all do the same thing. In the same way, even though we are many individuals, Christ makes us one body and individuals who are connected to each other. God in his kindness gave each of us different gifts. If your gift is speaking what God has revealed, make sure what you say agrees with the Christian faith. If your gift is serving, then devote yourself to serving. If it is teaching, devote yourself to teaching. If it is encouraging others, devote yourself to giving encouragement. If it is sharing, be generous. If it is leadership, lead enthusiastically. If it is helping people in need, help them cheerfully. Love sincerely. Hate evil. Hold on to what is good.

ROMANS 12:3–9 GW

- Has God given you the gift of giving?
- Has God entrusted you with more resources as a result of your giving, and if so, is that a sign that He would like you to exercise giving more often?
- Do you desire to be someone God uses to give to others?
- Besides giving financially, in what other ways can you give to others?
- Are you a teacher, a leader, or a person who builds others up and encourages them? How would God like for you to use that gift?
- What opportunities can you think of that God has given you lately to be generous to others? How did you respond?
- Is there something you're holding on to that you feel God wants you to give? What will it mean if you let go?

Father, You are a giver. You gave the greatest gift, Your Son. And I am so thankful to have received Him. Now I ask You to reveal to me what I can give to You and to others. I want to be a generous giver. Sometimes things in my past cause me to hold on to material things or make me less open to giving of myself to others. I refuse to let those past hurts and difficult experiences steal the joy of giving. Give me wisdom in where You would have me give. Show me the people You'd like for me to connect with and the organizations that need what You've given me to share. Thank You for the unique ability and talents You've given to me, even the ones I don't yet know about. Illuminate my talents and show me where I am to use them for Your kingdom purposes.

LIVING FROM THE INSIDE OUT

,,,

"I'm baptizing you here in the river, turning your old life in for a kingdom life. The real action comes next: The main character in this drama—compared to him I'm a mere stagehand—will ignite the kingdom life within you, a fire within you, the Holy Spirit within you, changing you from the inside out. He's going to clean house—make a clean sweep of your lives. He'll place everything true in its proper place before God; everything false he'll put out with the trash to be burned." Jesus then appeared, arriving at the Jordan River from Galilee. He wanted John to baptize him. John objected, "I'm the one who needs to be baptized, not you!" But Jesus insisted. "Do it. God's work, putting things right all these centuries, is coming together right now in this baptism." So John did it. The moment Jesus came up out of the baptismal waters, the skies opened up and he saw God's Spirit—it looked like a dove—descending and landing on him. And along with the Spirit, a voice: "This is my Son, chosen and marked by my love, delight of my life."

MATTHEW 3:11-17 MSG

,,,

- Baptism is a sign to others of your commitment to live for Christ. Have you been baptized?
- If you've been baptized, what does your baptism mean to you?
- While your spirit is immediately changed when you receive Christ, your human nature has to be taught to live in agreement with your spirit. What are some changes you have experienced since you received Christ?
- As you began to live from the inside out, what differences in your attitude occurred right away?
- What things took some time?
- What are you still working on?

Lord, thank You for the life I have today. I am grateful for the changes You've helped me make so far in my life. I know there are things I am still working on. I want my life to be an open book for others to read and see how much they need to know You. Forgive me when I fail, and help me to forgive myself. When I make a mistake, I will take responsibility for it. I will live my life according to the purpose You have for me. While I remember my old life, I also remember all the things You saved me from. You have made me new. When others bring up my past, please give me wisdom and courage to speak to them about the changes You've made in me. I want more than anything to point others to You.

TRUSTING GOD

██

At that time the disciples came to Jesus and asked, "Who, then, is the greatest in the kingdom of heaven?" He called a little child to him, and placed the child among them. And he said: "Truly I tell you, unless you change and become like little children, you will never enter the kingdom of heaven. Therefore, whoever takes the lowly position of this child is the greatest in the kingdom of heaven. And whoever welcomes one such child in my name welcomes me."…
Then people brought little children to Jesus for him to place his hands on them and pray for them. But the disciples rebuked them. Jesus said, "Let the little children come to me, and do not hinder them, for the kingdom of heaven belongs to such as these." When he had placed his hands on them, he went on from there.

MATTHEW 18:1–5; 19:13–15 NIV

██

- Do you have children? If not, do you want them?
- If you are a parent, what do you consider your responsibilities to God? To your child?
- What have you learned about your personal relationship with God because of the children in your life?
- How has your perspective on God as your Father changed because of your relationship with children? Do you see Him differently? If so, how?
- How important is it to you to bring the children in your life to God so that He can bless them? How do you do that? In prayer? In trusting Him to care for them when you're not with them?
- As a parent or mentor in a child's life, how do you bless them?
- What do you do to encourage them and build their faith?
- Do you often reflect on God's care for His children when you see a child loved and cared for? How does that make you feel toward your heavenly Father?
- How does having children in your life increase your trust in God?

*Heavenly Father, thank You for the children
You've placed in my life. Thank You for taking
care of them and teaching me more about
You as I grow in my relationships with them.
I realize my trust in You is not about knowing
everything or doing everything right; it's about
understanding that no matter what happens,
You will be there with me. You care for me like
I care for my children—and even more. Just
as they depend on me, I can depend on You.
You are with me. Help me to recognize the life
lessons found in my relationships with these
children. I want to see You, learn from You,
and understand myself better through the
daily exchanges with my children. Help me to
see them through Your eyes so that I may be
the leader, mentor, and parent they need for
each season in their lives as they grow in You.*

A BETTER MARRIAGE PERSPECTIVE

*And the Lord God said, "It isn't good for man to be alone;
I will make a companion for him, a helper suited to his needs."
So the Lord God formed from the soil every kind of animal and
bird, and brought them to the man to see what he would call
them; and whatever he called them, that was their name.
But still there was no proper helper for the man. Then the
Lord God caused the man to fall into a deep sleep, and took
one of his ribs and closed up the place from which he had
removed it, and made the rib into a woman, and brought her
to the man. "This is it!" Adam exclaimed. "She is part of my
own bone and flesh! Her name is 'woman' because she was
taken out of a man." This explains why a man leaves his
father and mother and is joined to his wife in such
a way that the two become one person.*

GENESIS 2:18–24 TLB

- How do you describe love?
- If you're not married but desire to be, are you growing in Christ so that you are ready for marriage when you meet your future spouse? How?
- If you're married, would you say you and your spouse love each other more today than when you were first married?
- Do you believe you are growing in Christ?
- How do you measure your spiritual growth individually and as a couple?
- What area of your marriage needs the most work on your part?
- What are you doing to work on that area?
- What do you need from your spouse?
- What does your spouse need from you?
- Do you pray together?

Lord, I pray for my marriage. You know my heart and the heart of my spouse. You know the challenges we face. I know there are things I need to work on. I know there are things I can do better. Tune my ears to hear what my spouse is really saying. Open my heart to receive the words as words spoken in love. Help me not to become defensive when we have challenges. Show me how conflict can be beneficial to our relationship. Help me to respond in a calm and peaceful manner, even when I'm hurt or frustrated. Remind me, Lord, of the things that speak love in a way that expresses my heart. Show me what I need to do to demonstrate admiration and respect. Let us both show that we're each other's biggest fan. Help us to become a strong team working together to strengthen our marriage as we grow in You.

ETERNAL TREASURE

||||||||||||||||||||||||||||||||||||||||||||||||||||||||||||||||||||||||||||

But you are. . .A [special] PEOPLE FOR God's OWN POSSESSION,
so that you may proclaim the excellencies [the wonderful
deeds and virtues and perfections] of Him who called you out
of darkness into His marvelous light. Once you were NOT A
PEOPLE [at all], but now you are GOD'S PEOPLE; once you had
NOT RECEIVED MERCY, but now you have RECEIVED MERCY.
Beloved, I urge you as aliens and strangers [in this world] to
abstain from the sensual urges [those dishonorable desires] that
wage war against the soul. Keep your behavior excellent among
the [unsaved] Gentiles. . .so that for whatever reason they may
slander you as evildoers, yet by observing your good deeds
they may [instead come to] glorify God in the day of
visitation [when He looks upon them with mercy].

1 PETER 2:9–12 AMP

||||||||||||||||||||||||||||||||||||||||||||||||||||||||||||||||||||||||||||

- What does it mean to you to know that you've been chosen by God as His very own?

- Does the fact that God chose all of us as His own change how you see others?

- Next time you're in church, take a look across the room full of people with this perspective in mind. Do you see your church family differently?

- God values our lives in a completely different way than we value them. Does seeing others from an eternal perspective change your view of your purpose? And theirs?

- Does life look different because believers have an eternity of living to do beyond death in this life?

- We each have value, not because of wealth, knowledge, or the kind of vocation we choose, but because we belong to God. How do you see yourself and others differently knowing your worth comes from what God does, and not because of what we do?

God, this world is small compared to the vast expanse of who You are. It's so easy for me to confine myself to the four walls of what's going on in my daily life. It's easy to see people for what they do rather than for who they are to You. Help me to value each person with an eternal perspective. This world is not my home, and my time here is but a small sliver of time compared to eternity. Help me to live in Your truth, committed to the people I will spend eternity with. Help me value the relationships You've placed in my life and esteem people of all walks of life. May I see them as the eternal treasure they are to You.

THREE THINGS FOR SUCCESS

,,

"Be strong and of good courage, for to this people you shall divide as an inheritance the land which I swore to their fathers to give them. Only be strong and very courageous, that you may observe to do according to all the law which Moses My servant commanded you; do not turn from it to the right hand or to the left, that you may prosper wherever you go. This Book of the Law shall not depart from your mouth, but you shall meditate in it day and night, that you may observe to do according to all that is written in it. For then you will make your way prosperous, and then you will have good success. . . . Do not be afraid, nor be dismayed, for the Lord your God is with you wherever you go."

JOSHUA 1:6–9 NKJV

,,

- What is God preparing you for?
- Joshua, as second in command of God's people, spent decades observing God's relationship with Moses. Is there someone God has placed in your life for you to learn from?
- What lessons have you learned in your own seasons of preparation?
- Once Moses died and Joshua stepped into Moses' role, God used what Joshua had experienced to help him lead. He promised to be with Joshua as He was with Moses. What promises have you seen in the lives of your mentors that you believe God will also do for you?
- In what ways are you prepared for the task God has set before you? How have you developed courage along the way?
- Sometimes success requires you to obey God without all the details. When have you obeyed not knowing, and what was the outcome?
- Like Moses, Joshua knew God's commands. How does your decision to obey God's Word set you up to be successful?

Heavenly Father, You are preparing me for something more. I know it will be challenging and at times more than I think I can accomplish, but I don't have to do it alone. You are always with me. You've prepared me and given me great examples of who You are and what You can do when I follow You. I will be strong and courageous. I will hold fast to my faith. I will obey You even when I don't have all the details. I will read and study Your Word so that when I need it, it is there in my mind. Remind me of Your Word as I step into this next place You have for me. May it be a season where I lean on You, learn more, and lead others along the way.

LETTING GO OF CONTROL

,,,

*[God] planned to bring all of history to its goal in Christ.
Then Christ would be the head of everything in heaven and
on earth. God also decided ahead of time to choose us through
Christ according to his plan, which makes everything work
the way he intends. He planned all of this so that we who had
already focused our hope on Christ would praise him and give
him glory. You heard and believed the message of truth, the
Good News that he has saved you. In him you were sealed
with the Holy Spirit whom he promised. This Holy Spirit is
the guarantee that we will receive our inheritance.
We have this guarantee until we are set free to belong
to him. God receives praise and glory for this.*

EPHESIANS 1:10–14 GW

,,,

- Have you ever struggled with giving God complete control of your life?
- Do you ever hold on to certain things in your life in the hope that you can somehow make sure they go the way you want them to?
- Have you believed that if you give complete control to God, He'll make you do something you don't want to do?
- You know God loves you, but do you find it difficult to fathom that He loves you more than anyone ever could?
- Is it difficult sometimes to accept that God wants His absolute best for you?
- Are you struggling to hold on to something that God wants you to let go of?
- What are you trying to control today?
- What would it take for you to let go and give God complete control?

God, for many years I've believed that if it's to be, then it's up to me to make it happen. I struggle with letting others help me—including You—because I don't think it'll be done the "right" way. Forgive me. My way is only right in my own eyes. I believe You love me and only want Your very best for me. Sometimes I fear that Your best may mean I have to do things I don't want to do. But I am determined to let go and trust You. Whatever You ask of me, I will do. I am willing to step out of my comfort zone and experience all You have for me. It is the only way I can become the person You created me to be. Give me courage and strength to take that leap of faith, to go without knowing the destination. Today I choose to surrender and walk with You.

A DEEPER COMMITMENT TO PRAYER

,,

*Are you hurting? Pray. Do you feel great? Sing. Are you sick?
Call the church leaders together to pray and anoint you with
oil in the name of the Master. Believing-prayer will heal you,
and Jesus will put you on your feet. And if you've sinned,
you'll be forgiven—healed inside and out. Make this your
common practice: Confess your sins to each other and pray
for each other so that you can live together whole and healed.
The prayer of a person living right with God is something
powerful to be reckoned with. Elijah, for instance,
human just like us, prayed hard that it wouldn't rain,
and it didn't—not a drop for three and a half years.
Then he prayed that it would rain, and it did.
The showers came and everything
started growing again.*

JAMES 5:13–18 MSG

,,

- What if God only worked in our lives when we prayed?
- Would your prayer life look different? How?
- What would you pray for? And for whom would you pray?
- When you discover others are in the middle of a trial, do you offer prayer right then and there? If you don't, what would it look like if you applied your faith to their situation and prayed with and for them immediately?
- Why is it easier to pray for those who ask for it later instead of right then?
- Do you pray for them later?
- What changes do you want to make to your prayer life? What actions do you need to take?

*Lord, thank You that I can bring my prayers
to You and expect answers. Today it's not
about me but about those I know and love.
I pray for each one. You know the struggles
they have today. . .some need healing in their
bodies; some have broken hearts and need
restoration in their emotions. For those with
financial challenges, I trust You to meet their
needs and to provide for them in a way that
they recognize could only come from You.
Give me discernment and wisdom to
know who and what to pray for each day.
When someone says they need prayer, give
me the courage to step up right then and
join my faith with theirs to see You do the
miraculous that only You can do. Help me to
step up and lead in prayer in a new way.
I ask You for revival in the hearts of those
I know and love, as well as in my own heart.*

THE LORD DELIVERS US ALL

Blessed are those who have regard for the weak; the LORD delivers them in times of trouble. The LORD protects and preserves them—they are counted among the blessed in the land—he does not give them over to the desire of their foes. The LORD sustains them on their sickbed and restores them from their bed of illness.... " 'For I was hungry and you gave me something to eat, I was thirsty and you gave me something to drink, I was a stranger and you invited me in, I needed clothes and you clothed me, I was sick and you looked after me, I was in prison and you came to visit me.'... The King will reply, 'Truly I tell you, whatever you did for one of the least of these brothers and sisters of mine, you did for me.' "

PSALM 41:1-3; MATTHEW 25:35-36, 40 NIV

- Is it important to you to protect the weak? Why?
- If so, when did it become important to you?
- When were you weak in any area of life? Perhaps you weren't physically weak, but spiritually, emotionally, or financially weak.
- Who stood up for you? Was it God? A parent?
- How did their actions influence you?
- The enemy looks for those who are easy targets. What is the first thing that makes you spiritually weak?
- The Bible speaks of God's great concern for the weak, especially in Psalm 41. When was the last time you prayed for strength personally? How did God answer?
- Perhaps you're still navigating a difficulty that left you vulnerable. How is God's mercy covering you now?

Heavenly Father, thank You for Your concern for the poor and the weak. I appreciate the times in my life when I was poor or weak in one way or another and You ministered to me. You comforted me and sent Your people to encourage or help me in whatever way I needed. You also helped me to grow through those times, just as You will help me now. I pray for others I know who are struggling. Send whatever it is they need. Speak to people across this earth to support them. Cover them with Your mercy. Bless them and show them that You care. Give them peace and strength to overcome as well as the help they need to become stronger. Show me how I can help them.

READY OR NOT

,,

"Listen to me, all Israel who are left; I have created you and cared for you since you were born. I will be your God through all your lifetime, yes, even when your hair is white with age. I made you and I will care for you. I will carry you along and be your Savior. . . . And don't forget the many times I clearly told you what was going to happen in the future. For I am God—I only—and there is no other like me who can tell you what is going to happen. All I say will come to pass, for I do whatever I wish. I will call that swift bird of prey from the east—that man Cyrus from far away. And he will come and do my bidding. I have said I would do it and I will."

ISAIAH 46:3–4, 9–11 TLB

,,

- God is always; He is from the beginning to the end. What questions do you have for God about your future?

- He lived your yesterdays, your todays, and your tomorrows. What does it mean to you that God knows who you were, who you are, and who you will become?

- Even though God knows everything, He doesn't always share it with you. Why do you think that is the case?

- The Bible says God's ways are higher than our ways. Does that help you trust Him with your future?

- God knows the deepest questions of your heart. He also knows what you would do with the answers. Will you trust Him to give you the information you need in due season?

- How do you go about doing that?

- What is the hardest part of not knowing?

- How do you discern God's wisdom for your life?

God, it seems like life would be easier if I had all the answers. I have so many questions, and yet I want to trust You for the answers when it's the right time. I don't know what the future holds, but You hold my future.

As I grow in my understanding of Your character and nature, I will come to know You more. I will better understand that You love me more than anyone can. You have my best interest in mind. I'll try to follow You and not do things my own way. Give me a heart of discernment that I may know the way to go.

I tune my ear to hear Your voice, and I desire to live by Your commands. I trust You. My future is bright. The best is yet to come!

COURSE CORRECTION

,,,

*My soul dissolves because of grief; renew and strengthen me
according to [the promises of] Your word. Remove from me the way
of falsehood and unfaithfulness, and graciously grant me Your law. I
have chosen the faithful way; I have placed Your ordinances before
me. I cling tightly to Your testimonies; O LORD, do not put me to
shame! I will run the way of Your commandments [with purpose], for
You will give me a heart that is willing. Teach me, O LORD, the way
of Your statutes, and I will [steadfastly] observe it to the end.
Give me understanding [a teachable heart and the ability to learn],
that I may keep Your law; and observe it with all my heart. Make
me walk in the path of Your commandments, for I delight in it.*

PSALM 119:28–35 AMP

,,,

- When did you receive the Lord?
- What was that like? Were you alone or with others?
- As you received Christ, how did you feel?
- Salvation is a resurrection in your soul. How did (does) God breathe new life into you then (and now)?
- Have you ever lost sight of your salvation experience for a moment or two? Does it help you to remember what season of your life you were in and how your relationship with Christ has impacted you?
- How have you grown in Christ?
- What changes have you had to make?
- How do you look different, inside and out, to others? To yourself?
- What things are you working on to change today?
- How are you continuing to grow?
- How are you involved in sharing Christ with others?

*Jesus, thank You for saving me, renewing me,
and bringing me into the kingdom of God.
I am forever grateful for my new life in You.
May I never take my salvation experience
for granted. My life in Christ is not a one-
and-done experience. You are changing me
each day. Each day I need to grow in my
faith—in my relationship with You. Sometimes
a course correction is necessary. I lose my
focus and sense of direction at times. When
that happens, I invite You to get my attention
quickly and bring me back on course with You.
Shine Your light into areas of my life that are
stagnant. Show me the places in my heart that
need work. Help me to be courageous when
I know the work is going to be hard. Give me
the strength to do the work I need to
do so I continue to grow in You.*

ANSWERED PRAYERS
AND SECRETS REVEALED

,,

*Then the secret was revealed to Daniel in a night vision.
So Daniel blessed the God of heaven. Daniel answered and
said: "Blessed be the name of God forever and ever, for wisdom
and might are His. And He changes the times and the seasons;
He removes kings and raises up kings; He gives wisdom to
the wise and knowledge to those who have understanding.
He reveals deep and secret things; He knows what is in the
darkness, and light dwells with Him. I thank You and praise
You, O God of my fathers; You have given me wisdom and
might, and have now made known to me what we asked of
You, for You have made known to us the king's demand."*

DANIEL 2:19–23 NKJV

,,

- How do you feel when your prayers are answered?
- Daniel was in a tough place when he asked God for answers—his life depended on God's intervention. When have you felt God's answer was critical to your survival?
- Daniel depended on his friends to go to God on his behalf. Do you have a support system like that?
- Who do you turn to for agreement in prayer?
- Who do you trust to pray for you when you feel like you can't pray?
- When there seems to be no answers humanly, God's wisdom can provide exactly what you need. When has God come through for you like that?
- Once the answer comes from God, what has been your response? Are you excited, relieved? Do you want to rush out and tell everyone about it? Remember to take time to thank God for revealing secrets you needed to know.

God, You have all the answers. I recount the many times when I didn't know what to do. I remember the times when there were no answers. I remember when it seemed all hope was lost, and yet hope burned in my heart. And You saved me. You gave me insight into a situation that my human mind would never have thought of. You know my questions before I even ask. Thank You for Your wisdom and knowledge. Thank You for the people You've placed in my life whom I can count on to be there for me, to intercede for me and pray for me when I can't. In my excitement, remind me to take time to thank You and give You the glory for the answers.

DO NOT WORRY

"So I tell you to stop worrying about what you will eat, drink, or wear. Isn't life more than food and the body more than clothes? . . . Can any of you add a single hour to your life by worrying? And why worry about clothes? Notice how the flowers grow in the field. They never work or spin yarn for clothes. But I say that not even Solomon in all his majesty was dressed like one of these flowers. That's the way God clothes the grass in the field. Today it's alive, and tomorrow it's thrown into an incinerator. So how much more will he clothe you people who have so little faith? . . . So don't ever worry about tomorrow. After all, tomorrow will worry about itself. Each day has enough trouble of its own."

MATTHEW 6:25, 27–30, 34 GW

- What specifically are you worried about today?
- Most of the things we worry about never actually happen. Think about the things you have feared in the past. How many actually happened?
- Jesus promises us that He will take care of us. How can you show Him that you believe this promise if you are holding on to worry?
- How would your life feel different if you were worry-free? Ask God in prayer to take away your fears, and then be willing to let Him.
- Would you say that worry is a lack of trust in God? Why or why not?
- Worry can derail your faith like a train off its tracks. What helps you to refocus and get back on track?
- What else can you focus your thoughts on today so that you don't fall into the trap of existing in worry?

Jesus, You know my worries even if I never speak them out loud. Sometimes I allow scenarios to play out in my mind that derail my faith. I refuse to give the enemy a foothold in my thoughts. Forgive me for holding on to worry instead of trusting You. You are the source of all that I need, and more! When those worrisome thoughts play on a loop in my head, replace them with Your truth. Your grace. Your promises for life to the fullest. Remind me to go to Your Word and renew my mind with Your truth. Today I lay my worries at Your feet, Savior. You have promised to perfect that which concerns me. I believe You are at work on my behalf, working out things for my good.

COURAGE TO PRAY

‖‖

"This is what makes you so great, Master GOD! There is none like you, no God but you, nothing to compare with what we've heard with our own ears. And who is like your people, like Israel, a nation unique in the earth, whom God set out to redeem for himself (and became most famous for it), performing great and fearsome acts, throwing out nations and their gods left and right as you saved your people from Egypt? You established for yourself a people— your very own Israel!—your people permanently. And you, GOD, became their God. So now, great GOD, this word that you have spoken to me and my family, guarantee it permanently! Do exactly what you've promised! Then your reputation will flourish always as people exclaim, 'The GOD-of-the-Angel-Armies is God over Israel!' And the house of your servant David will remain sure and solid in your watchful presence. For you, GOD-of-the-Angel-Armies, Israel's God, told me plainly, 'I will build you a house.' That's how I was able to find the courage to pray this prayer to you."

2 Samuel 7:22–27 MSG

‖‖‖

- When God makes a promise, He delivers. What promises has God made to you?

- What promises has God already kept?

- When have you doubted God's promises? Why?

- What challenges your courage to believe God's promises for your life?

- When you find yourself doubting God, what restores your faith and gives you courage to believe again?

- Jude 20 (MSG) says, "Carefully build yourselves up in this most holy faith by praying in the Holy Spirit, staying right at the center of God's love." How do you do that?

- Prayer is a great time to remind God of His promises. Do you think God needs to be reminded? How does this benefit you?

*God, You always deliver on Your promises.
It's not so much that I doubt You as it is that
I doubt myself. I overthink things. I doubt if
I heard You clearly. Sometimes I struggle to
stand firm and believe. Help my unbelief. Help
me to recognize the enemy's strategies and
stand against his assault. I will be strong and
courageous, believing that all You've promised
in Your Word belongs to me. I build myself up
on my most holy faith today. I pray and expect
the Holy Spirit to strengthen and uphold me.
Today I remind You of the promises You've
made. I list them now and remind myself as I
speak about each one with You. I stir up my
faith today and believe I will receive all that
You have promised in Jesus' name.*

POURED OUT FOR OTHERS

,,

Preach the word; be prepared in season and out of season; correct, rebuke and encourage—with great patience and careful instruction. For the time will come when people will not put up with sound doctrine. Instead, to suit their own desires, they will gather around them a great number of teachers to say what their itching ears want to hear. They will turn their ears away from the truth and turn aside to myths. But you, keep your head in all situations, endure hardship, do the work of an evangelist, discharge all the duties of your ministry. For I am already being poured out like a drink offering, and the time for my departure is near. I have fought the good fight, I have finished the race, I have kept the faith.

2 TIMOTHY 4:2–7 NIV

,,

- Are you pouring your life into others?
- What image comes to mind when you hear the words *a life poured out*?
- How do you pour out your life?
- Are you mentoring others? How are you serving those God places in your life?
- God can use anyone who is willing. Are you willing?
- What excuses come to mind when you think of serving others?
- What is needed to step beyond those excuses and take action (if you have not)?
- Does this seem hard? Let's simplify it—it's merely sharing your life, your insight, your time, and your resources with others.
- Have you asked God where you should be serving? How has He responded? What's the next step?

Lord, I do want to serve others. Forgive me for the excuses I've used in the past and help me to see beyond them. While I don't see how I can possibly have time for others, I know that You have a plan. Thank You for those who have poured into me and given of themselves to teach me and help me grow. Show me now who You've placed in my life. Maybe it's not one person but a daily giving of myself with smiles and words of encouragement. I am willing to share my life. Open my heart to receive others, and show me what I have to give. Help me to grow in You as I take this next step. I'm ready and listening. Give me wisdom and discernment in who they are and how I am to serve them. I ask You for pockets of time to be a blessing to others.

GOD'S WORD, LIGHT IN THE DARKNESS

*Nothing is perfect except your words. Oh, how I love them.
I think about them all day long. They make me wiser than my
enemies because they are my constant guide. Yes, wiser than
my teachers, for I am ever thinking of your rules. They make
me even wiser than the aged. I have refused to walk the paths
of evil, for I will remain obedient to your Word. No, I haven't
turned away from what you taught me; your words are sweeter
than honey. And since only your rules can give me wisdom and
understanding, no wonder I hate every false teaching. Your
words are a flashlight to light the path ahead of me and keep
me from stumbling. I've said it once and I'll say it again and
again: I will obey these wonderful laws of yours.*

PSALM 119:96–106 TLB

- Have you ever been lost at night in the woods or experienced something similar? Perhaps your family went on a camping trip and you wandered too far from the campfire. How did it feel to be lost in the dark?

- The world we live in today can be a dark place, but the Bible serves as a light in the darkness. What scriptures from God's Word serve as a light in your life today?

- How do Bible truths keep you safe in the midst of this present darkness?

- How does God lead you?

- When it seems as if things are growing darker and darker, how can you flood God's light on the situation you're facing?

- How do you point out the light of God's truth for others to experience?

Lord, there have been many times when I was lost and You found me—from my salvation experience to each situation where I needed You to provide safety and protection. I live in a dark world, but Your light and life will always shine. There is no light that can't overcome the darkness. When I am tempted to shut my eyes and succumb to the darkness, remind me that Your Word is alive and active and that You are always with me. When I am unsure of the truth, shine Your light deep within my heart so that I can discern Your will and Your truth. Thank You for the truth of Your Word, a steady beacon in the darkness that always points me back to You.

LIFT UP YOUR LEADERS TO GOD

,,

I urge that petitions (specific requests), prayers, intercessions (prayers for others) and thanksgivings be offered on behalf of all people, for kings and all who are in [positions of] high authority, so that we may live a peaceful and quiet life in all godliness and dignity. This [kind of praying] is good and acceptable and pleasing in the sight of God our Savior, who wishes all people to be saved and to come to the knowledge and recognition of the [divine] truth. For there is [only] one God, and [only] one Mediator between God and mankind, the Man Christ Jesus. . . . Therefore I want the men in every place to pray, lifting up holy hands, without anger and disputing or quarreling or doubt [in their mind].

1 TIMOTHY 2:1-5, 8 AMP

,,

- Do you pray for leaders of your country, state, city, and church?
- Do you feel like you have influence with your leaders?
- Prayer gives you a powerful influence. Would you agree?
- Do you find it difficult to pray for leaders when you don't agree with the way they are leading?
- Is it easier knowing that God has asked you to pray for them?
- In addition to leaders, do you pray protection and blessing over your church, city, state, and country?
- How have you seen God intervene in those areas?
- What would you like to see God do for your church? For your city?

Heavenly Father, I declare that You are still God of this country. Many of Your people, like me, continue to stand in faith and believe that You protect and keep our country. I pray today for the president and national leadership of this country. Make a way for those who don't know You personally to come to know You now. Speak to their hearts and fill them with a love for You and for Your people. Thank You for my state and city government. May You use all of our leaders to bring prosperity and blessing to the people they serve. Give them wisdom beyond their years and strategies that will benefit us. I pray for my church leaders. May their hearts be opened to hear Your voice, and may they be compelled to follow each instruction You give. Fill them with compassion for people and a deeper love for You. May they teach Your truth in love; may they serve, inspire, and encourage us to love one another as You have loved us.

WHEN THERE ARE NO WORDS

*He was despised and rejected by mankind, a man of suffering,
and familiar with pain. Like one from whom people hide their
faces he was despised, and we held him in low esteem. Surely
he took up our pain and bore our suffering, yet we considered
him punished by God, stricken by him, and afflicted. But he
was pierced for our transgressions, he was crushed for our
iniquities; the punishment that brought us peace was on him,
and by his wounds we are healed. We all, like sheep,
have gone astray, each of us has turned to our own way;
and the Lord has laid on him the iniquity of us all.*

ISAIAH 53:3–6 NIV

- When have you or someone close to you experienced loss?
- When have you reached out for someone, longed for them to be there, and yet they were no longer there?
- Many times we think of death and loss together, but there are many other forms of loss—loss of a job, loss of friendships, loss of all things familiar when you move to a new city. What losses are you navigating right now?
- After loss it's easy to isolate yourself because of pain. Who do you trust most to share your pain?
- Jesus knows your sorrow, whether it's your own or empathy for a friend. When you feel inadequate to help a grieving friend, how can you push through and be there for them?
- Why is it important to give voice to your emotions?
- Have you asked God to help soothe a wounded heart?
- Is there something you've held back from saying to God? Why? Tell Him today. Jesus stands ready to help you through your sorrow. As you pray, express each feeling and imagine yourself giving that hurt to Him.

Lord, You already know how I feel, but it's important for me to say some things so that I can give them to You. Grief sometimes feels like fear—not the same but similar. It gives me those butterflies in my stomach. Others' voices seem muffled. It's hard to make out what they are saying. Focusing can be difficult. And then there are the feelings, the thoughts, and the wordless nothing. I need You to comfort me, to take away the pain. I need others to realize that it's okay to sit and say nothing. I want others to understand that silence between us says so much. Thank You for being there to hear me when I cry out, to understand me when no one else can. While I know my world will never be the same because of this change, I can experience peace. You are with me.

TRUSTING GOD WITH YOUR CHILDREN

*The woman conceived and bore a son. And when she saw that
he was a beautiful child, she hid him three months. But when
she could no longer hide him, she took an ark of bulrushes for
him, daubed it with asphalt and pitch, put the child in it,
and laid it in the reeds by the river's bank. And his sister
stood afar off, to know what would be done to him. . . . By faith
Moses, when he was born, was hidden three months
by his parents, because they saw he was a beautiful
child; and they were not afraid of the king's command.*

Exodus 2:2–4; Hebrews 11:23 nkjv

- Can you imagine having a child and knowing that the ruler
  of your country had decreed that he must be killed simply
  because he was a male? Moses' parents defied Pharaoh
  and hid Moses as long as they could, but finally Moses'
  mother had to courageously set him among the reeds on
  the river and trust God to take care of him.

- If you are a parent, can you imagine anyone loving your child
  more than you do? It's hard to grasp, but God truly does.

- There are seasons in your child's life when you have to let
  them go—when they start school, when they learn to drive a
  car, and ultimately when they set out on their own. Have you
  struggled with letting go of your child?

- Was it hard to leave them on their own, even if it was a short
  while? Moses' mother had no idea that her baby would be
  returned to her to nurse him for the daughter of Pharaoh, yet
  she trusted God. Imagine how hard that must have been to
  let go of that floating basket.

- What are you doing to prepare to let go of your child?

- What helps you trust God after you let go?

Heavenly Father, thank You for my beautiful children You have given me to raise. I do my best each day to raise them in a way that pleases You. I pray that they know You and will never turn from Your ways. Help me to give them biblical wisdom and understanding. Show me what they need to become all that You desire them to be. Give me words when they need answers. Prepare my heart when it's time to let go, even if it's just a little. Comfort me as I remember that You are with them always, especially when I can't be with them. May they love You more each day.

THE THOUGHTS YOU THINK

,,

*Don't fret or worry. Instead of worrying, pray. Let petitions
and praises shape your worries into prayers, letting God know
your concerns. Before you know it, a sense of God's wholeness,
everything coming together for good, will come and settle you
down. It's wonderful what happens when Christ displaces worry
at the center of your life. Summing it all up, friends, I'd say you'll
do best by filling your minds and meditating on things true, noble,
reputable, authentic, compelling, gracious—the best, not the worst;
the beautiful, not the ugly; things to praise, not things to curse.
Put into practice what you learned from me, what you heard and
saw and realized. Do that, and God, who makes everything work
together, will work you into his most excellent harmonies.*

PHILIPPIANS 4:6–9 MSG

,,

- Your thoughts are powerful. You become or act on what
  you think the most about. So what consumes your thoughts?
- Are there ever so many thoughts darting through your mind that
  you feel like you're having several different conversations?
- When you have negative, worrisome thoughts, what do
  you do?
- How successful have you been in shifting negative thoughts
  by consciously counting your blessings or reminding yourself
  of a Bible promise?
- What are you thankful for?
- What promises from the Bible are you holding on to today?
- Have you asked God about your thoughts?
- How does God help you manage your thoughts?
- What thoughts do you have that you need to change?
  Write them down so you can share them with God during
  your time with Him.

*God, sometimes my thoughts consume me.
When they are negative thoughts they can
steal my faith. I need Your help keeping those
negative, tempting, and worrisome thoughts
under control. So I give You authority in my
life to help me deal with my thoughts. Help
me keep my mind on You and on the promises
You've given me. When I forget, remind me
that my words have power, and when I speak
Your words from the Bible, I'm putting Your
words into my heart and mind. I'm thinking
about Your thoughts for me, for my life, and
for my future. I want to know Your words, Your
truth. I want to take those negative thoughts
and turn them around so that they become
positive, faith-filled affirmations. I will be
more diligent to pay attention to what I'm
thinking. I choose to think on the truth,
the reputable, honorable things.*

THE SECRET TO A CHANGED LIFE

It is God who produces in you the desires and actions that please him. Do everything without complaining or arguing. Then you will be blameless and innocent. You will be God's children without any faults among people who are crooked and corrupt. You will shine like stars among them in the world as you hold firmly to the word of life. Then I can brag on the day of Christ that my effort was not wasted and that my work produced results. My life is being poured out as a part of the sacrifice and service I offer to God for your faith. Yet, I am filled with joy, and I share that joy with all of you. For this same reason you also should be filled with joy and share that joy with me.

PHILIPPIANS 2:13–18 GW

- What do you do when you really don't feel like obeying God?
- God has not left you alone in your struggle to become all that He desires you to be. In what ways has God shown you that He wants to help you be successful?
- Do you find it easy to become sidetracked in your journey without the influence of godly mentors?
- Would you consider yourself someone God wants to use to mentor others?
- Why does your witness matter?
- While your spirit is immediately made new, it is the mind, will, and emotions that must learn to follow your spirit's lead. Have you found that as you do God's will (even when you don't really want to), the desire to do His will grows within you?
- How important is it to trust God to change your desires?

God, I want to continue to grow and change. I want to live a life that speaks of Your goodness and love. Let my words, my thoughts, and my choices be pleasing to You. May all that I do be a witness to others. Teach me Your ways and help me to obey You, even when I don't really want to. Sometimes the things You ask me to do are hard because I don't know all the details. I have to move forward in faith, trusting that You have a good reason for asking me to do this next thing. Give me wisdom and peace. The secret to change in my life is to give everything to You— to let go and let You work everything out for my good. Help me to stay committed to the journey ahead, and remind me that others follow me as I follow You.

HEALTHY MIND, WILL, AND EMOTIONS

Yes, because GOD's your refuge, the High God your very own home, evil can't get close to you, harm can't get through the door. He ordered his angels to guard you wherever you go. If you stumble, they'll catch you; their job is to keep you from falling. You'll walk unharmed among lions and snakes, and kick young lions and serpents from the path. "If you'll hold on to me for dear life," says GOD, "I'll get you out of any trouble. I'll give you the best of care if you'll only get to know and trust me. Call me and I'll answer, be at your side in bad times; I'll rescue you, then throw you a party. I'll give you a long life, give you a long drink of salvation!"

PSALM 91:9–16 MSG

- The battle for your well-being starts in the soul—your mind, will, and emotions. When has negative thinking put you on a different path from the one God wanted you on?
- Thoughts produce feelings that ultimately lead to your actions. Would you agree that whatever you think about most is eventually what you choose to do?
- Is it difficult to stay positive when things around you are discouraging?
- Adam, the first person God created, walked with God in the cool of the evening. How do you spend time with God?
- How does quiet time encourage you spiritually?
- What things fill your spiritual tank? A walk in the woods or a little time near the lake? Perhaps a few moments at the kitchen table with your Bible in the morning?
- How do you turn down the noise of your busy life? What works best for you?
- How can you quiet those thoughts that are contrary to the truth of who you know God to be in your life?

God, my life is so busy and so loud. More than anything, I know I need to spend time with You. It's important to revive my spirit with Your presence. I am fueled by the words You speak to me through Your Word. My spiritual battery is charged by praise music and time worshipping You. When I'm tempted to disconnect and become closed off from You, remind me that my health—spirit, soul, and body—comes from You. I choose to encourage myself in the truth of Your Word, in prayer, and in quiet time just thinking about who You are and the goodness of what my relationship with You means to me. I invite You to interrupt my busy life and remind me that I need to spend time with You.

ARISE AND SHINE

‚‚‚

*Before anything else existed, there was Christ, with God.
He has always been alive and is himself God. He created
everything there is—nothing exists that he didn't make. Eternal
life is in him, and this life gives light to all mankind. His life is
the light that shines through the darkness—and the darkness
can never extinguish it. . . . Arise, my people! Let your light
shine for all the nations to see! For the glory of the Lord is
streaming from you. Darkness as black as night shall cover all
the peoples of the earth, but the glory of the Lord will shine
from you. All nations will come to your light; mighty kings
will come to see the glory of the Lord upon you.*

John 1:1–5; Isaiah 60:1–3 tlb

‚‚‚

- Fear grows in the dark. What fears concern you today?
- How do you battle your fears?
- What tools has God given you to stand against the darkness in your mind?
- How does the truth of God's Word change your perspective when facing fear?
- When have you seen the light of God's truth shine in your life and push back the darkness?
- What can you do to shine the light into the dark corners?
- What words, phrases, or songs come to mind when you need encouragement to confront fear?
- Just as you sit in the sunshine and take in its health benefits, how is God's truth and light good for your stand against fear?
- When do you feel most empowered to rise out of the darkness?
- How do you let your light shine?

Jesus, Your light and life live in me. I am filled with Your truth. Give me strength and wisdom to choose to think on things that build my faith. Your words written in the Bible encourage me. I speak Your Word out of my mouth, and hope rises in my heart. I will stand against the darkness. I will fight fear with faith, knowing Your glory and truth will overcome the darkness. No darkness can withstand even a sliver of light. I choose to walk in Your light each day. I remind myself of what You have done for me and that Your gift of resurrection life pushes back the darkness. When I am tempted to allow the darkness to creep into my thoughts, remind me to shine Your light on those thoughts, knowing it will expel the darkness.

FUTURE HOPE

,,

*We speak about the mystery of God's wisdom. It is a wisdom
that has been hidden, which God had planned for our glory
before the world began. Not one of the rulers of this world has
known it. If they had, they wouldn't have crucified the Lord of
glory. But as Scripture says: "No eye has seen, no ear has heard,
and no mind has imagined the things that God has prepared for
those who love him." God has revealed those things to us by his
Spirit. The Spirit searches everything, especially the deep things
of God. After all, who knows everything about a person except
that person's own spirit? In the same way, no one has known
everything about God except God's Spirit.*

1 Corinthians 2:7–11 GW

,,

- We all have questions about the future and think we truly want the answers. If you knew just how many hours, days, and years you would live on this earth, would you change the way you live your life in any way?
- While God won't likely give you those details, He has provided wisdom through scripture about how to live all of your days. With that in mind, are you using the time He's given you wisely?
- Are you faithful each day with the things God has entrusted to you?
- How can you really make every minute count?
- Do you look to Him to lead and guide you toward His purpose?
- God has promised you a future and a hope. What are you truly hoping for—in this life and for eternity?
- Do you spend your time with eternity in mind?
- Sometimes it's important to stay in the moment. What moments do you cherish most?
- How can you make the most of moments like those in the future?

Heavenly Father, You hold my future in Your hands. Each day I have breath in my lungs is a gift from You. Forgive me for the times that my perspective has been on the minute at hand and the problems I face. I give myself to You. I trust You with my life and ask You to help me to make every minute count. Help me to step back and enjoy the precious times You give me with You and with those I love. Give me a big-picture focus. Let me look deeply at the things that really matter and gloss over those things that—in the long run—really are insignificant. Reveal to me the things that I need to know by Your Spirit. My future is not mine but Yours!

TOPICAL INDEX

STILL ONLY HAVE 5 MINUTES?
TRY THIS!

The 5-Minute Bible Study for Women

In just 5 minutes, you will Read (minute 1–2),
Understand (minute 3), Apply (minute 4),
and Pray (minute 5) God's Word through
meaningful, focused Bible study. *The 5-Minute
Bible Study for Women* includes more than
90 Bible studies that will speak to
your heart in a powerful way.

August 2018 / Paperback / 978-1-68322-656-7 / $5.99